# THE UNFORTUNATE DESTINY OF OUR PLANET

# THE UNFORTUNATE DESTINY OF OUR PLANET

LENNART WINGARDH

ARPress
ILLUMINATING IDEAS.
EMPOWERING VOICES

**ARPress**
45 Dan Road Suite 5
Canton MA 02021

Hotline: 1(888) 821-0229
Fax:      1(508) 545-7580

Ordering Information:
Quantity sales. Special discounts are available on quantity purchases by corporations, associations, and others. For details, contact the publisher at the address above.

Printed in the United States of America.
ISBN-13:      Softcover        979-8-89330-272-1
              eBook            979-8-89330-271-4

Library of Congress Control Number: 2024901511

*"This book is bringing to life the ancient End of Time prophecies of God as if they were pronounced today."*

Author Wingardh presents the results of his studies over the last forty years concerning the coming destruction of Earth based on religious prophecies. His interest began through reading the Holy Bible and the Jewish Torah. Both books contain numerous dark predictions for the end times as revealed by God directly, including the Book of Revelation that vividly portrays the end times and passages such as God's warning to the prophet Isaiah that the end would be preceded by a loss of sunlight.

Words of warning are also derived from the Qur'an. All three place an emphasis on the ways that Satan seeks to pervert God's commands. Volcanic events, earthquakes, and progressively worsening weather are mentioned in these spiritual works, phenomena that all readers can recognize as increasingly common. Wingardh notes an asteroid calculated to hit Earth sometime from 2023-2025, marking a schedule for absolute destruction. He reads scripture as God's attempt to signal his actions and his messengers, or "Warners," regarding future occurrences, urging them to accept his existence and improve their lives in preparation for the horrific prophecies that will soon be realities.

Wingardh is a Swedish American who was born in Cuba and has traveled extensively, bringing cellular systems to Latin America. His assertions regarding the end of time are arrayed in an organized and erudite manner, offering numerous scriptural references alongside scientific discoveries and the diverse writings of others, along with a few salient photographs. He has constructed this wide-ranging work as both an alert and an encouragement to readers, exhorting them in a closing statement to secure for themselves "a place in the Kingdom of the only Living God." Wingardh's book will doubtless be studied and discussed intensively by open-minded readers striving to better understand planetary changes and their ultimate, dreadful purpose.

*- The US Review of Books*

# CONTENTS

The Book is dedicated to the Only Living God.

the All-knowing, the All-seeing,

the Almighty Creator and Owner of Everything.

After extensive research I found that

God's prophecies were about the Global Warming,

why it's happening that it's taking Planet Earth to its end,

to take place in our generation.

God began to reveal this matter in His ancient Prophecies

beginning almost three-thousand years ago,

through the Prophet Isaiah, something nobody ever

understood. The book will hopefully be of benefit

for those in need of Guidance!

# INTRODUCTION

D ear Reader, writing an introduction - that obviously depends on the subject at hand - can be very complicated, as in the case of the prophecies of God. I became interested in His prophecies some forty plus years ago, when I began to bring together information about the subject. I couldn't in my wildest fantasy have imagined the terrible destiny that lay hidden therein for us, the human species. It has taken me many years of arduous work to reach the point that I can say I know what it was God foretold in His prophecies that's taking place now. The book provides detailed information explaining how our planet has entered into *"an irreversible process of devastation"* that's on course of taking mankind to its (our) impending eradication, as foretold by God.

I'm writing this book with the purpose of giving you the reader the reasons of why you, independently of faith, if any, or anything else, need to change your ways of living. The book provides ample information about the matter, and it will exclusively depend on you, what you do. I say however that missing out on making the needed changes will continue taking you on the way of perdition.

After penetrating into the depths of God's End of Time prophecies and as the result of my altruism, I say, *"Oh God, how extraordinarily horrific are the punishments You are about to begin to lash out upon mankind!"*

Despite that the book isn't about science fiction, the ghastliest horror fiction story pales in comparison to what God revealed about the punishments that are getting ready to be unleashed upon mankind. Reading what God describes in His prophecies gives the idea of a *Pandora's box of horrors*, from the ancient Greek Mythology.

In order to avoid copyright issues with the translations of Bibles and the Qur'an which would hinder publication of this book, I've re-written the issues at hand, providing similar but not copied texts. That will bring you straight into *"the unfortunate destiny of our planet"* that God foretold and warned about time after time in His prophecies.

In the Book of Revelation Chapters 8 and 15, we find out how terrible it's going to get at the End of Time, when God lashes out in his intense anger against a wicked disrespectful mankind.

In the Jewish Torah, Book of Numbers Chapter 12:6, it's said that God gave His prophets visions of occurrences HE saw would affect Planet Earth and mankind in a remote future. This gives an idea of *the extraordinary capabilities of God, Our Creator!*

Through His Prophet Isaiah, known as 'the prince of His latter prophets', and through newer prophets, God warned that the sun would no longer shine when the End was nearing.

It took time before I realized that God didn't give Isaiah and future prophets the understanding of His visions. Because it seems that they didn't understand what God showed them in the Visions – the prophets wrote what they thought the visions described – not the specific End of Time occurrences shown in the Visions that would lead to the shattering of our planet. God did not create the occurrences of what was in the visions. HE showed His prophets our future (devastation) as HE saw it taking place, when the sun would no longer be seen as the atmosphere darkened. Doubtless, the darkening skies, preventing the sunlight to shine through, were the effects of future volcanic eruptions darkening the skies. What a coincidence that (as we see reported on the internet) more and more volcanoes are awakening all over the planet.

It occurred to me to study the Qur'an, not because somebody told me to do it, but because of a specific matter related to the powers of the mind. Amazingly, I found much more than I expected to find, which drove me to penetrate more and more into its depths. It's a remarkable book that's a must to read, wherein God addresses a host of subjects and very extensively about our End.

I learned that the Qur'an was authored by God, called "Allah" in Arabic. Therein I learned that God transferred the texts of the Qur'an – "Al-Qur'an" in Arabic - through His archangel Gabriel - to His prophet Muhammad, an illiterate man who – it has been recorded - met with the archangel Gabriel thousands of times to orally transfer the Qur'an.

God talks at length in the Qur'an about His creation of Adam and of the becoming of Satan, describing who he is. HE warns *"the children of Adam"* – us – about Satan – who HE defined as *"our sworn enemy"*. Note that God doesn't call us His children.

In learning how much God mentions Satan in the Qur'an, I found it surprising that He wouldn't have said anything of significance about him – our Nemesis and most significant enemy - in the Jewish Torah, His original Law.

I'll return to this matter in chapter 2 that's dedicated to bringing out in the open who Satan is and how he has managed to fool and deviate the vast majority of mankind away from God, of which HE warns about repeatedly.

Through His Prophet Jeremiah 8:8 in the Jewish Bible, God said that His Law (that was what HE called the Torah) had been changed by scribes (different Bibles have different names for who HE said did it). This awestruck me because it means that at least a part or parts of the Jewish Bible became corrupted.

God repeatedly foretold (prophesied) that our End would be caused by the evil behaviour of mankind that in turn would set in motion a multitude of effects of devastation, some of which would be supernatural in nature. As the result of my studies, I say it has already been set in *motion resulting from effects of the man-made global warming*. The worsening weather, the increase of earthquakes, and the many volcanoes increasingly coming to life around the globe are tangible signs of a planet visibly in trouble.

For thousands of years God's prophecies remained impenetrable because nobody was able to unveil what they meant. It was for the reason that until the global warming (its effects) were in place (as it is now) there was nothing against which to compare His prophecies. The effects caused by the global warming are forcefully changing the dynamics of Planet Earth, something that was practically untouched for thousands of years. Now, it's a different story.

The atmosphere, which has been and continues being perturbed by the mostly man-made poisonous greenhouse emissions, has affected the oceans in ways unprecedented - warming them - beginning with the industrialization in the mid-eighteen hundreds.

Scientists didn't have the slightest idea of what was going on and the havoc it was causing to the oceans, affecting and changing them and our planet! It began slowly, unnoticeably, changing their temperature and currents. Worst of all is the melting of the vast ice sheets and glaciers by the warmed-up oceans, which wasn't thought possible to happen as fast as it's occurring with continuously increasing speed.

Reports on the internet, such as this one that reads, *"glaciers are melting faster than previously thought"* and one that reads *"Greenland's ice is melting at a rate scientists thought would be our worst-case scenario in 2070,"* tell a very bad story because the acceleration of the ice melt is real and, can't be stopped.

It's important that we realize that it is the warmed-up oceans - not the atmosphere - that's causing the glaciers and the vast ice sheets in Antarctica and Greenland to melt. According to NASA reports, the ice-melt is speeding up at an exponentially accelerating rate! I ask, has any scientist figured out how to put a stop to that?

Earth scientists need to come to grips with themselves and realize that even if all emissions to the atmosphere were stopped instantly and it became completely cleaned – which is impossible - the atmosphere has already caused so much damage to the oceans – as can be observed from all the reports on the internet – that it doesn't matter from the perspective of the oceans what happens up there.

Mankind - it's an inevitable fact, as we know - will continue to spew out greenhouse emissions to the atmosphere, increasing the damage to it and the oceans for the time that remains for our planet. On top of that there are those giga-tons of methane gas that are being freed from melting permafrost that adds to an already bad atmosphere! Since the damage already inflicted to the oceans - that will continue to increase - is beyond repair, efforts to reduce the emissions to the atmosphere are a waste of money and resources.

Sometime ago a report came out on the internet endorsed by around eleven thousand scientists, who indicate in regards to 'climate change' that *'we have a clear and equivocal emergency'*. How good that they finally realized it! But they still haven't realized that there's nothing to do about it, as this book provides evidence of.

We need to learn that *we, mankind – us unknowing* - put in place *the most lethal weapon of mass auto-destruction ever produced*, which is in the process of driving our planet - once and for all - towards our annihilation, as was foretold by God. We know it as the *industrialization*, the one that caused the global warming, also known as climate change, the harmful effects of which are irreversibly driving our planet towards devastation.

God's End of Time prophecies are definite. What HE foretold was what HE saw taking place that can't be changed. There is not going to be another opportunity, which God foretold through Isaiah telling us that *"Planet Earth will be made uninhabitable"*. The revelations HE made through Isaiah, that we wouldn't be able to see the sun any more, means – as I see it - that volcanic eruptions will become commonplace everywhere, filling the skies with ashes and dark poisonous smoke. I'll return to this matter in sub-chapter 8.7.

In regards to what's happening to the oceans, refer to article by Harvard Professor Mitrovica and Professor Bamber at the University of Bristol, UK, titled *"The U.S. has caused more Global Warming than Any Other Country"* on the internet on January 22, 2015. Therein we learn what's in the process of happening. I'll return to this matter in chapter 8.

God made it clear in revelations throughout time that our foretold annihilation is being caused by the effects of the wicked evil actions of mankind, against each other and very notably against our "Mother Earth," but most important against Him. Look around! What do you see? It's a thoroughly corrupt world in deep crisis that's getting worse by the minute. In Latin America – which I know very well – corrupt, greedy presidents and their governments have become shamelessly rich by pilfering what is the *working capital* of their countries. The same thing is happening in many other countries, as well. The money rightfully belongs to its inhabitants, the ones who give their votes to elect their presidents, who steal it and take it away to accounts in foreign countries instead of putting it to work wherefrom it was stolen. With what right do the Presidents and their governments take advantage of their positions that its inhabitants gave to them?

The corrupt presidents and their governments' first priority to enrich themselves at the expense of the people is causing increased poverty and the disintegration of the societies, Venezuela, being one of the worst cases. Its inhabitants, who live in an everyday increasing misery, are desperately fleeing their country's lack of work, increasing criminality, and social injustice, resulting in an increasing exodus of people. Undocumented immigrants swarming into the USA and to other countries that are unprepared for that kind of 'invasion'.

Effects of wickedness of mankind are extensively caused by the wealthy who use their wealth and positions – starting with its presidents – to take advantage of the lower classes.

The effects of our actions - *what we say, do, and even think* - are 'governed' by God's *Divine Universal Karmic Law* of '*Cause and Effect*'. What it means is that '*what we sow, we shall harvest,*' from which there's no escape. We need to understand that the sum-total of the evil of a fast-growing mankind caused along the millennia is impacting our planet in more and more powerful ways.

This is highly appreciated by Satan, who influences the feeble minds of man to cause the governments to fail and fall in his nicely laid out traps of deceit. Satan is incessantly and methodically causing corruption and the disintegration of societies, taking with him most people to the abyss of Hell. In chapter 2 we shall learn that God said (as HE reveals in the Qur'an) that HE will fill Hell with all the people who 'follow Satan'.

I say, wake up, be aware, learn and change your ways of thinking and living!

I say again, be aware that every word that God ever pronounced is as valid today as when HE pronounced it, beginning with His Ten Commandment wherein HE says that HE is the only God, who must be worshiped. This is valid for all human beings, independently of what you believe.

In order to highlight the seriousness of our situation as we are getting close to our end, let's go back in time thousands of years ago. In the Book of Genesis in the Jewish Torah, it's written that God saw how wicked everyone on earth was and how evil their thoughts were. This is remarkable because it sounds as if HE was describing our current world.

After seeing what HE saw, God said that HE was going to wipe out the people that HE had created. As is written, God was pleased with Noah, who together with his family were the only survivors HE left alive after the deluge. At this time – now - however, God has declared that HE will make our planet uninhabitable and extinguish mankind.

An important objective of this book is to provide evidence that God, the only Living God, exists, that His prophecies of our end are real, and that they are coming to fulfilment. What's awaiting mankind is revealed in the Book of Revelation wherein we learn that *hail and fire mixed with sulphur is going to rain on the earth, which will cause it to burn down*. How and when it's going to happen; only God knows.

An asteroid known as 2018LF16, discovered by NASA in June 2018, has been calculated to be able to hit our planet in any of the years 2023, 2024, and 2025 which, I've concluded, is on schedule with the time when this revelation will be fulfilled.

How is it possible to know that we have reached the foretold End of Time? Reading this Book will tell you all about it.

The most important sign by far is the global warming, that's progressing far faster than anybody has imagined. It, and very specially the oceans will cause a series of enormously destructive effects to affect our planet and principally the coastal areas.

Scientists, need to learn the fact that status quo for our planet is that even if all *greenhouse emissions* to the atmosphere were instantly stopped and it becomes completely cleaned – which is an impossibility - the atmosphere will continue to increase to damage the oceans. This is so because the emissions to the atmosphere will continue to increase for the foreseeable future. The measurable result (by NASA) of this is the continued acceleration of the melting of the vast ice sheets and glaciers that's changing the oceans.

What's on course to happen to our planet can be compared to a snowball rolling down a mountain. It speeds faster and faster until reaching the end of the slope where it disintegrates.

The oceans – seventy percent of the planet's surface, all joined together as one body - is the *killer element* that began – many years ago - the process of bringing about the foretold devastation of our planet! Just imagine what will happen when all that water at some point becomes pushed to move in one direction, completely throwing Planet Earth off balance!

In chapter 8, our journey will take us through *the multiple effects caused by global warming* – which God warned about so many times - how it's on course to cause devastation to our planet and the extinction of mankind! You'll learn that Earth scientists have taken distance to religion – as denoted by a Harvard Professor in an article on January 3, 2015 in the New York Times, titled "Playing Dumb on Climate Change". It was a mistake because in doing so, scientists missed out to learn from the prophecies in the Jewish Bible and in the Book of Revelation wherein God described how Planet Earth would be devastated at the End of Time!

I want to go as far as to say that taking distance to His prophecies (messages) that were explicit warnings of God about the future destructive effects of the current global warming was a major offense against God on part of the scientists.

It's my sincere desire that this book shall help you to learn what's happening with our planet and create a much-needed *awareness* and *consciousness* of the fact that it's getting late and change your ways of being. This *awareness*, among many things, should be used to begin to plan for and put in place *emergency measures* for what actions to take when our planet begins to break down at any moment. Such as, for instance, what actions to take when great catastrophes occur such as the so-called "*Big One*" in California and along the whole West Coast, taking place most probably as *a triple whammy*, as it seems getting ready to do?

A suggestion to philanthropists – who support the rich and well-to-do – do it instead for the causes of God. You'll do it by helping the poor and needy, who are '*close to His Heart*'. Read the Book of Luke 16:19 in The New Testament and what Jesus said about "*The Rich man and Lazarus* (a beggar)". It'll give you who live in your plush homes surrounded by great wealth something to think about instead of thinking about how to become richer and how to outshine your next of kin.

In the realization that nothing of that will be of good when you move on to the Hereafter, begin to share of your wealth! Get involved helping the poor, the elderly (AARP), the sick (St. Jude's Children's Hospital), and so many others. In this way you'll create what God calls 'credit checks' to be redeemed in the next life. Avoid building up 'debts' that'll weigh you down in your 'soon-to-come' next life.

Rich people are probably laughing sarcastically, saying, "What a crazy guy, who does he think he is?"

I say, as God said to His angels, "*I know what you know not.*"

The enormous *stock market* fortune you think you own, will soon be an illusion. Your chance to do good to help the needy will have vanished. Your big loss won't be money, but that of where you end up in your Next Life, where Satan wants you to be! It's up to each individual what you do, but have in mind that it's your Soul's *eternity* you are playing with!

You who don't believe in this, denying that it's true, are free to do so. The free will that God gave to us allows us to do it. But denying what's every day more evident because you stubbornly don't believe makes Satan very happy! You'll surely remember this on *'the Day of Regret'* - described in chapter 1.

This book is bringing to life the ancient End of Time prophecies of God as if they were pronounced today. Our near-future looks to be ruinous as the effects of global warming speed up and become more destructive. At the same time that the most powerful countries are getting themselves armed up to the teeth to go to war as we see it happening with Russia who attacked Ukraine.

I spent many years and countless hours of in-depth studies and thought to write the book. Before taking off on our journey through God's prophecies and matters related to the End of Time – it's important to have in mind the following:

God exists – irrelevant of what you believe. HE is the Only Living God who created everything including you and me. HE is a strict demanding God, who put in place Laws that rule everything. Disobeying Him – His Ten Commandments – puts you *out of play* for acceptance into His Kingdom. Know that every word HE ever pronounced is valid today and forever! God has said that those who don't believe in Him - that HE is the only God that exists - are *unbelievers* and *transgressors* who will be severely punished!

Satan exists – independently of what anybody believes. It's vital that you understand that the very moment you disobey God, as the result of accepting to do what Satan whispers to you to do, it's the first step you take that leads to Hell. It's of the essence to learn that there's no alternative. It's either up to Heaven for a few, or down to eternal suffering in Hell for the great majority of mankind.

God has said - Jeremiah 23:23 - that HE is everywhere and not in one place only. HE will help anybody who turns to Him in his heart, worshipping only Him, asking for forgiveness and guidance to help you to find the way to Him. Don't think that you can fool God because HE knows and sees everything and can't therefore be fooled!

Satan is everywhere on our planet, doing his utmost to make you fall in his traps of deceit, away from God. God has given you permission to follow him as you please to eternal suffering. It's remarkable that mankind wasn't made aware of this. I believe that this is the way how God tests each one of us.

In Qur'an 2:213 God indicates that in order to enter Paradise every individual must go through trial. There's no exception. In addition to this, in Qur'an 2:155, God says that HE will *test the steadfastness of every* individual (believers only) who HE finds worthy of being tested by Him while here on earth. This is a truly remarkable revelation about what it takes to be taken into account by God even before reaching Judgment Day, testing our worthiness to enter Paradise.

I'm sharing the knowledge I've acquired in the hope that it will help you to become one of the ones who choose to walk '*the narrow straight way of God*' - that implies to make '*sacrifices*' in this life - as it may seem - that will be well worth their while when we go on to a new life, when life here on earth comes to an end!

Before getting into the matters of *The Unfortunate Destiny of our Planet*, I want to provide some information about me. This is to give you an idea of my aptitude to take on complex matters such as the prophecies of God.

I am Swedish and also an American citizen. I was born in Cuba in July 1934 (long before Castro) where I went first to a Catholic nun's school close to home and later on to the renowned De La Salle School in the city of Santiago de Cuba, where I lived until age eleven. My father died from a wrongly applied influenza shot just before Christmas 1941.

Something remarkable occurred to me at age six which I believe defined my destiny, to one day take on to work with the prophecies of God. It happened an evening when I was praying, when a voice spoke to me saying, "*Lennart, don't pray to Jesus* (as Christians are taught). *pray only to God.*" That was it. After that, my worship was only to God. I remember thinking that, "*It's much better to pray directly to God.*"

In mid-October 1945, a few months after the ending of World War II in Europe, my mother, two smaller sisters, and I boarded a Swedish freightliner by the name *Sparreholm* destined to go to Sweden. After one day at sea, we hit a hurricane that lasted eight days. The waves were terrible (?) at about forty feet or more above or below the ship.

Something truly amazing happened when the ship entered the eye of the hurricane. the American North Atlantic fleet, suddenly appeared on the opposite side of the eye on the way back home after the war, '*Mission Accomplished*'. I remember that they and my ship exchanged light and flag signals. It was an incredible sight and a unique memory for life.

In Sweden, I obtained my formal education in telecommunications and in business administration. I took a two-year contract with the Swedish Royal Navy to get into their renowned telecommunications school and became an expert on its radar systems.

My dream was to someday return to Latin America that is why what I did in my youth was geared towards that goal. The first part of my dream and goal I attained in 1959 when I began to work for Ericsson, the Swedish telecommunications giant, at its head office in Stockholm in the sales and marketing for Latin America. My dream was fulfilled when I soon after was assigned to travel to introduce the Ericsson systems in Latin America. In mid-1967, I was sent with my family to Colombia as an ex-patriate. I decided to use my vacations to travel there with another Swedish cargo ship named *Venezuela* with my family.

We were in the midst of the English Channel in heavy fog when I noticed that the ship had stopped moving. I asked one of the crew what was going on. He told me that the ships radar had stopped functioning. When I told him I was a radar technician with the Swedish Royal Navy, I was immediately given access to the ship's radar. In less than an hour, I had the radar up and running, which allowed the ship to take up speed and move on. Curiously, the Johnson Line didn't send me a note of thanks. Now, was this a matter of destiny to be back on an identical Swedish cargo ship twenty-two years later with my expertise that allowed me to fix its failed radar? I believe God somehow made it happen.

In mid-1970, I reached yet another goal when I was promoted to the position of general manager for Telefonos Ericsson de Mexico in Mexico City. In late 1975, my first spouse became ill and died while in Mexico which caused me many upheavals. I cut short my contract and returned to Sweden with three young kids. By mid-1979, despite that I didn't have another job, I resigned from Ericsson and left. I wanted to do something different.

Within a matter of weeks, I flew from Stockholm where I lived to Helsinki, the capitol city of the neighbouring Finland, to meet with the management of the Finish elevator corporation KONE. I had sent KONE my resume or curriculum in response to an ad in a Swedish newspaper. They were searching for a general manager for a new subsidiary in Caracas, the Capitol City of Venezuela in South America. It was a country I had visited a few times and liked. Liking the country was an important factor in my decision to accept the job, something that would give me many headaches. But, as I've realized, it became my *trampoline* to continue to move towards my destiny to one day take on the prophecies of God.

KONE's management *grilled* me about my experience while filling me in about their newly acquired company in Caracas, I thought it sounded as if it was having many problems. What I learned left me wondering whether I should take the job. But before I knew it the CEO said, "Lennart, welcome to KONE." I remember thinking, "*Lennart, what have you gotten yourself into*?" I had a bad gut-feeling and wasn't happy.

When I arrived in Venezuela a month later after training in Finland and Brazil, I found the situation in Caracas to be chaotic (not as bad as now, but still bad). While in the cab from the airport to the hotel, I observed that high-rise construction activity was paralyzed, so no elevator installations. It also meant that the elevator sales business was at a standstill, which was bad news because it meant there were no new sales and no installations of sold elevators. So, from what would the company live? It was an impossible situation for the KONE Company, the smallest of eleven local elevator competitors. My early gut-feeling back in Finland had been confirmed.

I made up a business plan and sent a long telex informing Management in Helsinki about the situation. A few days later the Finns came to review the situation and found out their mistake to buy the company. I told them I would stay my one-year Contract to help the company. On the 1st of July 1980 I flew to the U.S.A. where I experienced my first 4th of July in Washington D.C.

Soon thereafter, I flew to meet with Motorola in Schaumburg in the outskirts of Chicago, Illinois. The V.P. in charge of Latin America, had invited me to come and see him. He had prepared an agenda for me to meet people in his organization and in a new cellular group just in the process of being formed within the communications sector. Before the day was over, I had a job as director of sales and marketing of special radio systems for Latin America that was set up specifically for me. The special radio system was the 'embryo' (not a ready product, still in process of development) to become what was called the North American AMPS (Advanced Mobile Phone Service) analogue cellular system.

Quite obviously nobody had an idea of what lay in front and how cellular would develop - I say - to become the most dynamic system of anything ever developed.

My most significant undertaking during the 1980s was the introduction of this system, which I pioneered into Latin America. In Argentina, I became known as "*the Father of Cellular* ". In Brazil, I helped the regulatory authorities at the Ministry of Communications in Brasilia to put in place the new regulations for the forthcoming cellular systems. I also helped the regulators in Mexico. In time, my activities in Latin America would translate into billions of dollars in the sales of cellular systems.

I also went to Spain and one of my most significant achievements was a contract I obtained from Telefónica in Spain. Management had viewed it as a *mission impossible* which I snatched away from Ericsson, my former employer, something they never expected to happen. I still keep the Letter of Intent to Motorola as a fond memory that was made out in my name.

In mid-March 1992, I had had enough of an unprofessional treatment on part of Motorola. I resigned and was again without a job. I flew to Stockholm, Sweden, where I had obtained an appointment with Mr. Kurt Hellström, Executive VP and General Manager of Ericsson Radio Systems. I had been able to get the meeting through my old buddies in high positions at Ericsson. As the result of my extensive cellular experience that caused his organization to lose a mayor cellular system's contract in Spain, he employed me. A new position was created for me, as director of cellular systems marketing support for Ericsson's subsidiaries in Latin America. The office was in Dallas, Texas, where I still live. I went into retirement in 1998, when I initiated my in-depth studies of the prophecies that had begun to interest me years before.

To round up, I'm a multicultural, multilingual person, fully fluent in Swedish, Spanish and English. I also speak German (my mother's language) and Portuguese, the result of countless visits to Brazil to meet with the Brazilian regulatory authorities and with Telebras, a 'holding company' of the government for its operating telephone companies.

To give an idea of how active I was, I flew somewhere around six million miles including with the defunct Pan-Am, Braniff, TWA, Viasa (KLM), and Eastern Airlines.

Now, you ask, what does any of that have to do with prophecies? Nothing! But it gives the idea of the active individual I was; always on the go, taking initiatives, developing new businesses in many countries in the region. I applied the same methodical approach to learning God's prophecies as I did in the businesses I worked with; being systematic, methodical, analytical, and perseverant, asking God to guide me before every meeting and thanking Him afterwards for the guidance and ideas, HE doubtless gave to me as in the case of writing this book.

Before I get going with the story, I want to again stress that this isn't science-fiction. What you'll learn is the truth of our unfortunate destiny, as foretold by God, not just once, but many times as warnings! His revelations of our future are complex making them extremely difficult – almost impossible - to understand. As the result, I had to put in an enormous effort to learn what HE was saying. The book describes how God's revelations of the extinction of mankind, that HE revealed through His prophets – as described in the Jewish bible - is on the way to reach fulfilment now, in our generation!

God doubtlessly had a purpose that one learns about when reading the Jewish Bible with an open mind. HE addressed His Jewish people to give them - as I believe - the opportunity to react and wake up and to alert all peoples of the need to change our (for Him) unacceptable wicked ways of being; which as God mentions in the Qur'an didn't happen.

I was intrigued by the prophecies and asked myself why God had issued them and why HE had brought up the matter so many times, both in the Scriptures and also outside of Scripture, that address the End of the World (our planet). How would our end happen? What was it that would cause the world - our planet - to reach the by God foretold devastation and our extinction engineered by a mostly wicked mankind? I had to find out!

I believe God wanted mankind to know that our time was counted. But the knowledge HE gave to His Jewish prophets in visions was to be kept hidden until the end was at hand, as many signs are showing it is. I'll revert to this matter, many times.

Natural phenomena, such as hurricanes, earthquakes, tsunamis, and a marked increase of volcanic eruptions are becoming more frequent and potent. Keep in mind the hurricanes that caused devastation in the Caribbean, Texas, Florida, and Mexico in 2017 and the *ice-bomb* hurricane Grayson that hit the East Coast beginning in the year 2018 and the one that hit North Carolina. And many more hurricanes that followed causing devastation in Florida.

Volcanic eruptions are becoming commonplace. many of those under the oceans have the potential to cause highly destructive tsunamis; the result of impending ruptures of subduction zones, such as the Cascadian subduction zone off the Northwest Coast of the U.S.A. I view this as one of many ripple effects of global warming. This is the beginning of what awaits us as our planet (Mother Earth) lashes out more frequently and with more extreme strength – giving back, so to say - for how we have treated her.

The discovery of NASA in 2018, as reported on the internet, that the ocean floors are sinking under the pressure of the added ice melt waters is bad news. Very amazingly, what hasn't been mentioned in any report is that the uneven distribution of the melt waters will cause the pressure on the ocean floors to be much greater in some locations than in other, increasing the risk for potential earthquakes and ensuing tsunamis at those locations.

This book discloses **why** and **how**, and approximately **when** (very soon) mankind will disappear - as God foretold - when Planet Earth becomes devastated, the result of our wicked actions! As mentioned before, this isn't something people believe in, but it happens to be the truth, as you'll find out. The effects of global warming – the 'pay-back' for our wicked actions - is in process - full speed - to cause our demise.

The effects of the current global warming were foretold many times by God, beginning close to two-thousand-eight-hundred years ago. That was when God for the first time revealed – through His Prophet Isaiah 13:10 - that in the days leading to our end, the sun would not be seen. This sounds like the effect of heavy global volcanic activity – something that has been on a steady increase. God told Isaiah to write that *the earth will be made lifeless, as it was before the creation.* How could this be? It so happens that there exist numerous revelations (prophecies) of God telling exactly what would (in an advanced process to) happen to our planet. However, nobody ever understood what God was revealing because, as mentioned, HE disallowed His prophets the proper understanding.

If you don't believe in God and His remarkable prophecies (*what HE revealed in them*), I assure you that reading this book with an open mind will change your thinking about many things – independently of your beliefs. If you don't believe in God and don't obey His commandments, it's plainly your problem, not His.

In the Jewish Bible, revelations to His Jewish prophets of our future – especially through Isaiah and Zephaniah are appalling. As mentioned, God repeatedly warned about the extinction of mankind. Refer to sub-chapters 1.15 and 1.16 in this book. In Isaiah 26:20, we learn that the LORD is going to punish the people (mankind) for our sins. In Isaiah 24:1 and 3, we learn that the LORD is going to devastate Planet Earth, leaving it uninhabitable as it was before His Creation of it. I'm sure that you agree with me that this puts in place a discomforting scenario of what God revealed would happen to us. Unfortunately for mankind, nothing has improved because His words revealing our eradication haven't changed!

What's in the process of happening becomes confirmed – as I see it - when we bring into the picture what I call *non-scriptural prophecies* made by seers of recent time. That's very especially the case with what Edgar Cayce – known as *The American Sleeping Prophet* – voiced. What he said about a hundred years ago, ties perfectly well in with what God revealed in His ancient prophecies wherein HE *foreshadowed* what would happen in a distant future – the one that has arrived at our doorsteps.

It was first when I read what Cayce said that I began to understand the ancient prophecies. Cayce undoubtedly was a seer to whom God – there's no other way – gave the gift to *see* our future. I came to realize that the terrible occurrences that Cayce described – to occur in our time - went *hand-in-glove* with the ancient End prophecies of God.

What Cayce said about the devastation of our planet was unfortunately never taken seriously and was ultimately forgotten. But, as the saying goes, "*Laid card lays*!" I believe that what Cayce saw in his séances - which was written down word by word by a secretary - was what God *made Cayce to see* and warn us about. There's no other explanation, so that's why "*it's on the table*".

Cayce wasn't taken seriously, as I see it, because nobody believes that somebody can foretell our destiny. The fact is however, that the scenarios Cayce foretold (that aren't at all clear in the ancient prophecies, for the reason indicated) tell precisely what's due to happen. I'll get back to

Cayce's prophecies in chapter 5, where we shall review in detail what he said and how amazingly well that ties into the ancient prophecies that God had His prophets (messengers) pronounce as warnings. Most important is that what he said ties extraordinarily well into current climate change reports that appear on the Internet.

How does the Qur'an (Al-Qur'an in Arabic) fit in? In reading texts in the Jewish Bible, I found that God's ancient prophecies and stories therein are complemented by the Qur'an. But as is written in the Book of Revelation, one must receive *wisdom* to attain the needed *understanding* of what's going on in the Revelations of God.

God gave this subject great importance in the Jewish Bible that I'll be dealing with it in chapter 1. As we've learned, the ancient prophets (God's messengers) were unable to understand the visions that God had given them. The meaning of the prophecy of the '*stars falling down to earth*' that was repeated by God through several of His prophets was to be kept sealed and secret until the End. I believe that that's why God made Cayce to *see and give us advance notice of* how our impending End will take place. I'll revert to what this revelation really means.

God revealed that HE would keep the time for the End hidden or secret. This is a revelation worthy of note that God makes in the Qur'an, Chapter 20:15. Therein God reveals how HE attracted Moses to the burning bush to talk with him. It was the first time Moses met God, who made him His first prophet. God told Moses that the end of mankind would take place in a distant future. But HE was going to hide when it would happen in order that every human being should receive his reward according to what he had achieved while here on earth. Note that God, the Author of the Qur'an, said this to Moses approximately in 1320 BCE, about 3,340 years ago. But, about two-thousand eight-hundred years ago, God began to warn (in His so-called prophecies) about future disasters, beginning with His Prophet Isaiah as mentioned before, to whom I will return in Sub-Chapter 1.15.

The global warming of the atmosphere - or rather its resulting effects that have been affecting the oceans - is irreversibly changing their temperatures and currents, as well as – worst of all is – *the rapid uneven upsurge of the ocean levels*! What it's doing, something that scientists never touch upon, is that it's causing a growing instability to the rotation of our planet around its axis. The instability growth will continue until Planet Earth is so imbalanced that it will be forced to change the location of its current rotation axis, something God warned about many times, beginning close to three-thousand years ago. Through the Prophet Zephaniah 1:18, God said that *'life will come to a sudden end'*.

Before taking off on our journey, I want to again underline that every Word that God pronounced through His Jewish prophets and in the Qur'an is immutable - valid forever - for all Eternity! The question to ask is, what does God think about mankind? The answer to this matter was revealed by Him many times in the Jewish Bible. As in Isaiah 24:5-6, wherein we're told that we *have broken the Laws of God*. The result was that God pronounced a curse on our planet. Through Isaiah, God said that mankind was going to pay for its wickedness. We need to be aware that God NEVER withdrew His curse. Therefore, it stands as when HE pronounced it.

In what I regard as one of the most remarkable revelations of all, in Isaiah 6 God reveals that HE dulled the minds of the people (those who don't believe in Him) and took away their sight and their hearing. This means that there are few people who have the needed understanding of matters of value that will continue to be this way until the End of Time. I'll return to this remarkable revelation of God.

Through my in-depth research of the reason for the prophecies in the Jewish Bible, I found that God always directed Himself through His prophets (His messengers or spokespeople) to the Jewish people (the Elders) - and only to them. Despite that, parts of the Jewish Bible became corrupted, as God revealed in Jeremiah 8:8, reading the stories of the prophets with an open mind provides understanding of all that went on between God and the prophets of His 'Chosen People', beginning about three-thousand years ago.

You say, "That was so long time ago." Well, that's how you see it. But for God, the Creator who lives in His Holy Place, time doesn't exist as it does for us. To reach this point has taken me many thousands of hours of dedicated work to learn and understand *what's in play*.

God made no secret of His anger and had His prophets (messengers and warners) to write many times that HE was not just *angry*, but even *furiously angry*, not only with His Jewish people, but with mankind. HE had many reasons to be angry. One of them must surely be the dishonesty of the Jewish and Christian priesthoods who HE reveals in the Qur'an, misappropriate money that's given to them to support their respective charity activities.

Preachers picture God as a benevolent being who, they say, loves us. The question is, is the picture of a benevolent, loving God true? I say that that unfortunately isn't true.

As is known, churches and synagogues are 'businesses' calling on their parishioners to fill their coffers (pockets), raking in *hefty cash-flows*. Since God knows everything – HE can't be fooled. HE knows what money is used as it should and what money is misappropriated. In the Qur'an 9:34, God reveals that priests (Christian) and rabbis (Jewish) take money that doesn't belong to them and use it inappropriately, which will cause them to be punished.

We learn about *the feelings of God* in Isaiah 24:1, who wrote that the LORD is going to devastate our planet. In the Qur'an, God reveals that HE told his Chosen People to pass on the knowledge HE gave to them to other peoples - something they never did. HE must have been terribly *frustrated* and must have said things like, "*Wake up* you *@#%&*." I can think of many words for what HE probably thought, *such as, "Why aren't you listening and following My (God's) warnings of what will happen to you in the future?*" God tried many times until it's evident - that after His Prophet Jesus became badly treated by the Jewish priesthood - supported by the people - God no longer *talked to them*.

God's revelations of our future are frightful – once we understand what HE was saying that we – mankind, the architects of our destiny - are on course towards a future of destruction and our eradication. That future has arrived and is now at our doorsteps, knocking at the door.

Articles are frequently found on the internet about how the ice melt in Antarctica and Greenland are in continuous acceleration, unstoppable, irreversible. As we've learned, there's only one thing that could cause this phenomenon, namely the warming oceans, which are melting away the vast ice-plates and glaciers everywhere. The Global Warming is affecting our planet with no cure. How do I know? It's precisely what I learned from God's prophecies - wherein HE described our future - which I'm in the process of sharing with you.

God didn't reveal anything that describes the initial stages of a future global warming – where we are now. HE repeatedly warned of it to the people HE called *His Chosen Jewish people*. Unfortunately for mankind, the Jewish people had no desire to share their knowledge of what would occur one day as God told them over and over - *in fulfilment of His revelations*.

We need to become aware of where our planet is headed, to gain awareness about our foretold destiny (the one that can't be changed), and so alter our individual ways of being and *become the Spiritual Beings that God intended us to be!*

Before I continue, I want to say that more than anything we need to realize that our sinful behaviour for several millennia has displeased our Creator. This is what's taking us to our self-inflicted auto-destruction. People spend time and tons of money in social gatherings at music and movie festivals such as the Oscars, sports events, and at other happenings to celebrate a horde of divas, stars, and idols who are revered by their fans. In other words, it's people celebrating people instead of taking time to worship God (in our hearts) and thanking Him for our lives. The problem, however, is that the people who preach about God don't know Him and therefore present erroneous pictures of Him.

Then there's the TV, the cellular systems, Facebook, YouTube and countless apps bringing far worse than good into our homes and lives, especially for the young ones. God, being all-knowing and all-seeing knows – as HE reveals in the Qur'an - that those are *useless pastimes* and a waste of time - that serves no purpose to prepare us for life in the *Hereafter*.

What is this? Who did ever say anything of the need to prepare ourselves for a life after death? Does it really exist? I say, if everybody is spending all the time with many different pastimes, how can anybody have time for anything serious? Look around you, especially in restaurants, I bet you that out of ten people, eight have their eyes stupidly affixed on their cell phones. Today's advanced radio frequency systems fill the airwaves in ways unprecedented, messing up the harmony of our planet and providing a multitude of programs that serve no purpose.

Seriously, when do you take time to turn to and worship and *'celebrate'* our Creator? Most people never do - which is to the detriment of those who don't worship Him and only Him in the heart as HE demands and has commanded! I'll revert to this matter in sub-chapter 1.11 titled, *"God warned against making our lives a pastime"* – spending time and money uselessly with no thought of the *soon-to-come Hereafter. The Hereafter* is the *everlasting* life for which God has said – we need to prepare ourselves in this life. There's little time left why *tomorrow* may be too late.

As I've mentioned, I began to read the Qur'an purely out of interest, finding numerous revelations of God wherein HE described Satan and how he came to be and that he (Satan) told God that he *"would stand in the way of mankind"* – and that - *"not many shall remain on Your (narrow) Way."* It astonishes me as indicated that very little of what God reveals in the Qur'an about Satan - who he is and how he came to be - is mentioned in the Jewish Torah that God called "His Law".

There isn't the least doubt that Satan, man's declared nemesis, one way or the other made sure the disclosures God must have made in the Torah about him, *describing who he was (is)* became eradicated. There isn't either one word of what God reveals in the Qur'an *that Satan said he would destroy mankind.* Satan without a doubt caused the Jewish priesthood to remove essential revelations of God from the Torah. In doing it, Satan could take on to do his evil works of deceit without mankind being aware that he was real and that he was driving mankind towards *its downfall* and *everlasting suffering*! In chapter 2 we shall find out how it happened.

Even if I quote the following verse of Nostradamus in chapter 5, I want to bring it in here because it will prepare you, providing an appalling nightmarish view (written around the year 1,550) about what the end time will be like, food is to be scarce in accordance with its author.

# Quatrain by French clairvoyant 'seer' Michael Nostradamus.

"Tears, cries, and laments, howls, terror

Inhuman heart, cruel, black,

making man shudder with fear. Blood to be shed,

hunger for bread and cheese, to none mercy."

# CHAPTER 1
## GETTING TO KNOW OUR CREATOR - THE ONLY LIVING GOD

At first view, this Chapter may seem odd with its differing sub-chapters, but herein I'm bringing up matters that introduces us to God, a Being Who has lived for 'Eons' of time, so extraordinarily unique and powerful that HE can't be described.

As we're learning, there exist numerous ancient Prophecies of God that are related to our foretold End-of-Time Destiny.

The Prophets were told to seal the Prophecies - as was the Prophet Daniel - by the archangel Gabriel, who told him to close the book and seal it until the end. Gabriel went on telling Daniel that many people would try to understand, which was to be in vain. In Sub-Chapter 1.2, I'll discuss the vital matter of Understanding.

Biblical scrolls with God's End-of-Time Prophecies were to be sealed and kept secret until the end as we learned before from Qur'an 20:15, wherein, as mentioned before, God told Moses that the time of the End would be held secret.

You'll find that I repeat the Prophecies and Revelations of God wherein HE foretold what's going to occur with us and our planet, which I do to underline and for you to remember the importance of His Words.

In setting up and discussing the matter, we shall get the scenario, so to say, to obtain the knowledge relative to the reasons for God's repetitive End-of-Time Prophecies.

God issued them frequently to warn us that unless we changed our (wicked) ways of living, we were doomed. Before continuing, it's vital to learn what God said through His prophet Isaiah, wherein HE teaches that "*HE is the Only Living God - besides Him there never was another God – and never will be*". It's very clear!

Herein God established - not only to the Jewish people – but to mankind as a whole - that '*HE is the Only Living that ever existed.*

The question arises, why would HE – the Almighty Creator of everything - accept the intrusion of any other God if there had ever been one? From where would any other god have come?

Given the enormity of His powers, it's impossible that HE would have accepted for any other God to co-exist.

Man-made Gods are mostly by man hand-carved idols or icons. Satan induced the ideas of such gods in the minds of religious leaders to make them and their followers to fall away from the only Living God!

God exists and lives in His Holy Spiritual Dimension of which we know nothing. His Powers are beyond the possibility of any human being to fathom. HE needs only to imagine something (anything) and by uttering the word 'Be' it becomes. HE can 'see' into – what we call 'the past' as well as 'the future' – which for us hasn't happened.

I want to round up by saying that 'if I don't take time to worship God, why should HE take time to do something for me!'

Anything we do, say or even think brings into action God's Karmic Law of 'Cause and Effect'. Worshipping God, brings it into action - as I see it - at its highest possible level of remuneration, meaning that '*what I sow (my worship and what I do), I shall reap the absolutely best possible harvest, as reward*'!

## 1.1 GOD – AND THE PERSPECTIVE OF TIME

Why is this important? It is very much so, because of what's written in Genesis 1 in the TORAH - that addresses the time-frame for God's Creation – that says – 'it took Him Six Days '– plus a seventh Day (Genesis 2) for rest; which we shall examine against what God has stated in the Qur'an, that God Himself Authored.

As we know, man's Time-count is fixed around the Movements of Planet Earth. 24 Hours to rotate around itself to fulfil One 24 hour Day, and 365 Days plus a fraction to make one rotation around the Sun in one Year. That's it. It's fixed and easy to count, and it goes on and on.

But, what about God's time count? Does HE have one? God has nothing in His Exalted Spiritual Realm that's fixed. HE is The Sovereign Everlasting God, who was, who is and will exist forever. Also, Past and Future, as they exist for man does in all certainty not exist for God, who lives in His Holly Place.

God's Creation according to the Qur'an, 11:7 reads, "*HE is the one who created the heavens and the earth in six yome* (periods)..."

In Qur'an 22:47 it is written that a Day of God is equal to a thousand years.

Based on this, God, the Author of the Qur'an made it clear that each Day of His is equal to a '*time-period* ' that spans a thousand man-years and probably more. The Arabic word used - 'yome' (or 'youm') – can mean not only a day or days but any amount of extended time period and even eons of time.

For God, a day of man is a microscopic fraction of time in the Eternity. When we analyse what's stated in Genesis 1, we find the following, that's said matter of fact.

At the end of each 'Creation Day,' it's said that "night passed and the morning arrived. It was the 'X' day."

This doesn't 'sound' as God saying it. Some Rabbi instead of the word "period" wrote "day" (doubtless caused by Satan to do it). However, this 'typo' (that didn't occur by error) happened, it has created confusion because it gives the impression that God made His

Vast Creation (each part of it) in one day – i.e., within twenty-four hours).

This matter is clearly one of debate, why we need to get a Perspective of differences between the known fixed Time-count of man and the one of God in His Exalted Spiritual Realm – of which we know nothing.

Why is this important – you ask? It has to do with the Prophecies – His '*Messages of Warning*' – which God made over and over – through His Jewish Prophets (His Messengers and Warners).

God gave extensive knowledge to His chosen Jewish people, who God ordered to share with mankind (in accordance with what HE declares in the Qur'an, to which I shall get back).

HE clearly tried to alert the Jewish people (all in vain) of '*occurrences*' *that I call 'of immeasurable consequence to the destiny of mankind* ', to take place in a distant future. That 'distant future' has finally caught up with us – as signs around our planet are signalling – giving evidence that it has arrived!

Not only did God foretell long ago about future devastating occurrences, HE also described the different kinds of scenarios of what was to take place on Planet Earth thousands of years later; and there where quite a few - all caused by the (for Him unacceptable) wicked doings of not only His 'Chosen People' but of mankind, as a whole.

The Warnings of God issued to His Jewish Chosen People - of occurrences to take place at the End-of-Time – were, as it looks - never understood by them. Current, what I call 'Signs' around us, however, point to the fact that the foretold occurrences are in an advanced process of taking place. The narratives in the Books of some Prophets – describe the occurrences, as they saw and understood them.

When we look back in time, for instance to the time of the Prophet Isaiah – close to 2,800 Years ago – it's impossible for anybody, except for God, to know what happened then, other than by reading the ancient Narratives in the Jewish Bible. But as I've found the use of very old language makes it difficult to make sense of and understand what the Jewish scribes described!

The oft-repeated Messages of Warning were made by God through who HE called '*His Warners*' – His Jewish Prophets ('*Messengers*')

– directed to His chosen Jewish people - wherein HE foretold and warned them – that unless they changed their ways of being – rebelling (as HE said) against Him - and obeyed His Commands and LAWS as HE gave them to Moses – the foretold events would occur in some distant future, at the End of Our Time.

It's evident – as I see it - that God '*saw*' what would happen to our Planet Earth someday – because, how else could HE issue His warnings of future devastation – and that it would take place as the result of (caused by) appalling changes to our planet's Atmosphere, so severe that '*the sun would no longer be seen*'. Today's Global Warming must be what HE was warning us about.

HE foretold precisely the kinds of Effects that would hit and devastate our planet and mankind. We have no way of knowing or understanding how HE could (can) know about our Future although HE has declared that HE is 'All-knowing' and 'All-seeing, and that nothing can be hidden from Him.

I've spent a countless amount of time to figure out the Prophecies. I'm convinced that God, in observing my determined indefatigable interest and effort to learn, has given me access to and revealed to me some of His Secrets related to our destiny. I believe this, because how else could I've been able to put in place the very different narratives contained in this Book.

## 1.2 THE VITAL MATTER OF 'UNDERSTANDING'

I say that the *'matter of Understanding'* has never been viewed as something that requires a special analysis. But, after spending countless hours trying to come to grips with it, I state that it is so important that it should have been looked into long time ago.

In both the Jewish Bible and in the Book of Revelation, as well as in the Qur'an, God has revealed that HE decides *"who receives 'understanding' of a particular matter."*

To have *'Understanding'* when working with God's Prophecies – is a must – especially with those related to His 'End-of-Time' revelations. But only individuals who believe in Him and obey His Commandments, will receive the wisdom that's needed to have the understanding of specific matters (such as for instance of the Effects of the Global Warming).

Without been given 'understanding' it's impossible to make the proper interpretation of the meaning of His Prophecies, as also in the case of many other matters.

The lack or absence of 'understanding' of a multitude of subjects - which God has taken away from most of us - has far-reaching consequences that may affect our correct judgment of just anything we deal with on a daily basis.

Now, this sounds strange and scary. Why is it this way and how can I validate this anomalous matter?

After reviewing God's revelations related to this subject, I state that this is one of the most important Revelations ever made by God, to which nobody has paid attention, because nobody ever realized that anything wasn't right.

But God mentions this in the Jewish Bible and in the Book of Revelation, and followed it up in the Qur'an, thus, there's no room for misinterpretation.

To underline the importance of this matter, I refer to the Introduction to the Britannica Atlas where it's said that *'Educators have indicated that - a deep gulf – often (I say, most of the time) separates the knowledge of something - from the understanding of it.'*

This is a remarkable declaration, but I state that the Educators in all probability haven't the slightest idea of how right they are and why it is this way.

'Understanding', as we are learning, is uniquely a gift from God, which comes out very clearly from what HE has revealed in the above-mentioned Books, as we shall find out.

It's as the educators have stated because I haven't been able to find even one individual, who has said anything of value, to explain what God revealed in His 'End-of-Time' Prophecies!

The many things that God revealed through Isaiah, reviewed in Sub-Chapter 1.15, are remarkable. The problem is obviously that nobody believes it.

In the Book of Isaiah 6:10-11, we learn that God empowered Isaiah to *remove the ability of 'the people'* (us) *to understand'*.

When Isaiah asked God, *how long it was going to be like that,* His answer was that it would be until the cities were uninhabited and the land deserted. In other words, forever.

I recommend reading Isaiah Chapter 6 in the Jewish Bible (or the Old Testament). The Message God gives therein is extraordinary, because it's of fundamental importance for mankind as a whole, relative to *'the matter of the understanding'*. Rather it is to learn why most people lack a needed 'understanding'.

What I'm saying in all probability sounds strange, and even bizarre to say the least. But it is what God has revealed in the above-mentioned Books.

The most clear-cut example that exits relative to this matter – I believe - is that of the voiced general negative attitude of Earth Scientists to use Religion (the End-of-Time Prophecies made by God, which are found in the Jewish Bible) in their Scientific Research work. Because of this – God, as I believe – has disallowed them to poses the needed understanding of what's happening to our planet - how it - in accordance to His Prophecies, is moving towards devastation.

However, and despite of this, I'm convinced that if Earth Scientists had taken interest in reading the Prophecies, wherein HE warned about the future - what could only be effects of the current Global

Warming - they could have had a different perspective and mind-set to this important matter!

In all probability, they would have been better of interpreting and having a better 'understanding' of the matters that God talked about in His many Prophecies (Warnings) of how and why it was going to happen; especially what was going to happen to Planet Earth through the Effects of the current Global Warming, the initial stage of which we doubtless have entered.

They would have learned - as mentioned before - that what God foretold can't be changed for the simple reason that the situations presented in His Visions, was what HE had seen irreversibly taking place around our planet.

What we learn from this - which is of fundamental importance - is that God made it impossible for people who don't believe in Him, and all the wicked ones – the vast majority of mankind – '*to understand His remarkable Prophecies (warnings)* about our end.

In the Qur'an Chapters 2:7, 4:155 (the second half) and 6:46 (the second half) it's written that, HE has sealed their hearts and their hearing, and has covered their eyes – taking away the understanding of all disbelievers - those who don't believe in Him in their hearts, for which HE says, they are going to be severely punished.

To most people the above in all probability sounds ludicrous. I suggest you go to the Internet and type in the references I've provided to learn what God has said. Then type in Book of Exodus, Chapters 8 to 14 to learn how God punished the Egyptians, which gives a clear idea of His extraordinary Powers.

The idea that any and all religions are good is completely erroneous. In the first of His Ten Commandments HE declared that HE is the Only God who must be worshipped. Nowhere anywhere has HE said that HE has a son who has to be worshipped – Nowhere!

The only one who wants mankind to worship Jesus, is Satan, believe it or not!

## 1.3 THE ESSENTIAL QUESTION WE MUST ASK

Do the Words of the Everlasting Eternal God, wherein HE expressed His
anger against mankind – Still Apply?

The answer is a resounding – YES! Why shouldn't they?

God's Words - His LAWS and everything HE ever pronounced are
'Eternal' 'Everlasting' 'Unchangeable'.

HE could, of course have changed what HE said, but mankind has
not given God any reason – as far as I know - that would have made
Him want to change what I call *His 'Sentence of Total Termination'
of mankind.'*

Therefore, about two thousand and eight hundred years later, God's
*'Sentence of Termination' of mankind* is as valid as when HE pronounced
it through Isaiah; and through later Prophets. Man (each one of us)
will be recompensed (mostly punished) *'according to our past deeds,'*
as is written in Isaiah 65:7. There's no escape or *'rapture'* (that was
invented by some Christian Church leader – induced by Satan to do
it). How would that happen? Nowhere has the LORD God mentioned
any such thing through any Prophet – **Nowhere!**

With his wicked 'rapture' idea, Satan again deceived the so many
times misled Christians – to fall farther away from God!

It is as Jesus said to his disciples, *"It's easier for a camel to get through
a Needle's Eye than for a rich man* (for mostly anybody really) *to enter the
Kingdom of God"*. This is especially so, for those people who don't obey
God's First Commandment to worship Him, and only Him. To be
complemented by doing good deeds and helping the poor and needy.

We need to understand that – as mentioned - for God time doesn't
exist, as it does for man. HE lives in His timeless Spiritual Realm,
where present, past and future, as we know it, doesn't exist.

God, who knows and sees everything, has known for 'eons' of time
*what's coming to mankind* (which we have caused to ourselves).

HE warned His Chosen Jewish People, over and over again, to
no avail, because they didn't (try to) understand His so many times
repeated Messages of Warning. As a result, the vast majority of mankind
will go one and the same way – down the pit of Hell!

I think these ancient Prophecies – that it's apparent - have caught up with us, will 'catch' attention.

I suggest reading the mentioned Bible passages to get an understanding of why God will (is ready to) punish mankind.

It was the first time God pronounced these kinds of Apocalyptic Prophecies of doom - which HE would repeat through His newer Prophets to come - and most notably by Daniel and by John from Patmos – and by God Himself throughout the Qur'an.

There's one fundamental question I want to bring up, which is - how come the Jewish People never '*picked up*' that there must be something severe involved. How come (my reflection) God '*took time*' with all those similar Prophecies - His Messages to them - over several Hundred years? There's No Answer! Maybe HE will say, that HE warned them (His Chosen People), but they were too busy to pay attention to Him. Such as in Isaiah 65:1 wherein it's written, the LORD said that HE was ready to answer the prayers of His people. And, that HE was ready for them, but they didn't try to find Him. One can easily understand why God became angry.

The answers to 'why', but more importantly today of 'how' it's going to happen, are being provided in this book; that will take you, as I mention in the Introduction, on an Odyssey - so dreadful - that the human mind won't accept that we're in effect reaching the terrible '*End-of-Our-Time*'.

There's no misunderstanding because all the facts are provided herein - for everyone to read and learn.

*The seeds for my interest* to learn about matters related to the *End of the World* (our planet) - were sown in 1981, when I acquired a book titled '***Prophecies & Predictions*** – *Everyone's Guide to the Coming Changes*', by Moira Timms, now gone. It's one of the best I've read on the subject. Thanks, Moira!

Before continuing, I want to mention that in the same way that passages in the TORAH became changed (mostly eradicated) as revealed by God through His Prophet Jeremiah in the Jewish Bible (Old Testament); the same thing happened as well with the original texts of the New Testament and the Book of Revelation, which were changed.

Satan, the Nemesis of mankind, managed to deviate the truth by which so many are being taken away from the Narrow Way of God.

Be aware that most of the Jewish Bible (Old Testament) texts are valid. Stories from the past, which provide Histories of past occurrences from that time, are unimportant. Large portions of what are revelations of God, continue being as valid as when God Pronounced His words.

Some of the 'Old Stories', especially the Exodus of God's Hebrew People from Egypt, led by His Prophet Moses, and later on by Joshua, provide insights of the Extraordinary Powers of God.

In the Book of Joshua in the Jewish Bible, we learn how God supported His Chosen Jewish people when HE opened up and made a pathway through the Jordan River (as when HE opened the Red Sea) making it possible for many Hundreds of Thousands of Jews to walk across its bottom totally dry, which must have taken many hours.

Still, another amazing recorded showing of His Immense Powers was when HE made the massive (viewed as in-destructive) walls of the City of Jericho to tumble down, leaving its inhabitants defenceless against the Hebrews who killed all its inhabitants by orders from God.

It's important to understand that God ordered the Jewish people to kill thousands and thousands of pagans, and not leave even one of them alive, the inhabitants of the cities that had been established in what was called 'the Promised Land' that God had promised to Abraham for his descendants. God sent His angels to help the Hebrew people destroy and kill the pagans, beginning with the mentioned city of Jericho, and on-going.

A parallel to this action of destruction ordered by God took place close to Two-thousand years later, around the year 630AD. It occurred when the Prophet Mohammad went out in Arabia to introduce God's new religion known as Islam. He met strong opposition from the pagan tribes against who he made war, destroying them, often against an overwhelming majority.

# 1.4 ARE GOD'S ANCIENT END-OF-TIME PROPHECIES STILL VALID?

In His ancient Prophecies God 'foreshadowed' for mankind cataclysmic occurrences – that would take place - in what was then – a Distant future - close to three-thousand years ago. The foreshadowing was made by God who sees everything in the past, current, and future, most surely as humans see things that are in front of us. Basically, as we today see distant occurrences on TV.

Again I say, be aware that every word ever uttered by God is valid as if HE had said it this very moment.

I believe that God was giving mankind the opportunity to acquire knowledge about the future of what we – mankind - have been causing through the ages, resulting from our wicked actions.

The problem has been our lack of knowledge of what it was all about since the Jewish people didn't share the teachings that God gave them – to be shared - as they had been told to do by God. I'll return to this matter.

Prophecies – is a subject that always caused interest – and resulted in many so-called documentaries of the Nostradamus prophecies, of the five-thousand-year-old Maya Calendar that ended on December 21st, 2012, and many others, such as the movie '2012' shown at the end of 2009. Additionally, there were the so-called Documentaries on the History and Discovery Channels – that were Science Fiction movies - that provided absolutely nothing of value, other than that of being modestly entertaining.

While the movies were packed with scenes of extreme destruction, nowhere was there an effort made to get to the heart of it all – to explain 'the reason' for God's Prophecies.

Why are the ancient Prophecies important? Many people probably don't believe they have Real messages of occurrences that will happen to us and to our planet? I've found that they are real and that they have (were made with) a purpose. If we pay attention, the Prophecies (Messages of God) were pronounced by an astounding amount of unrelated so-called Prophets? Why did God persevere so much in doing it?

This is a subject in which not many people believe or understand – that this book will unravel!

God's Prophecies – what HE *'foreshadowed, foretelling our End'* were *'explicit messages of warning'* – from God to who HE called *'His Chosen Jewish People'*. God pronounced His Messages through His Prophets (His *'Messengers'* or *'Spokespersons'*) through who HE warned of future disasters. Observe that there's no divination involved, as the word 'Prophecy' may suggest.

They were explicit messages, repeatedly foretold – to alert and warn the Jewish 'Chosen People' - that it needed to change, what HE called their increasingly rebellious wicked ways. In Isaiah 1:2-5 *God said that the people had rebelled against Him, making their wickedness burn (Him) like a fire!*

**Why, how and when will the End occur?** As much as we may not want to believe it 'The *End of our Time is upon us'*. The critical questions to ask are: **What's** the reason for it to happen? **How** will it occur? And, **When** (approximately) should we expect it to take place? *And, 'what do I need to do, to save my soul?'*

The time-frame for when the end will take place comes out with quite some precision when all Prophecies are compiled (brought together). The Chart in Chapter 6 brings together all Prophets and shows the Interrelation between their Prophecies.

I've found that - terribly for mankind – the foretold ancient Prophecies are in a *'fast accelerating lane of progression'* to be carried out. More so, the matter is continuously being substantiated by Scientific Reports related to a worsening Climate Change, i.e., the Global Warming – and especially to what its Effects have been (are) causing to the Oceans – *'the Mechanism'* that's in an *'Advanced Stage or Process'* of taking our Planet to its End.

*Climate Adaptation Is Essential, Scientists Warn,* a report to learn from. https://www.ecowatch.com/climate-change-adaptation-2531570965. html

This is something I will discuss in detail in Chapter 8 wherein I will provide evidence on how many of the occurrences that God forewarned about are already in place, and in an advanced process to begin to devastate our planet.

What's extraordinary, as mentioned, is that God began to describe the future End-of-Time occurrences as far back as close to Two-Thousand eight hundred years ago. God foreshadowed advanced effects of a future (current) Global Warming – that's keeping many Scientists busy trying to figure out what's going on. I say to them, read the Prophecies of God in the Jewish Bible! But as it seems, God disallowed them the proper understanding of them.

At this time, several what I call 'Signs' are calling out, clearly portending the imminence of the 'End-of-Our-Time'. I will return to what the 'Signs' are all about.

What to say about the Prophetic Maya Calendar, the End-date of which was December 21, 2012? Why did that most intriguing calendar - that spans five thousand years - finish abruptly on that day? As we observed, nothing happened. *But, did nothing really happen?*

I strongly believe that '*the end-date*' of the Maya Calendar – signalled – not an end, but, '*the beginning*' of a distinctly different and very short 'new era' – that was never before – and won't occur again. It began on December 21, 2012. The matter was most probably not revealed to the Mayas – reason for which they didn't integrate it into their calendar. The End of the Maya Calendar should thus be viewed as 'The *Beginning of our End*' – to take place in our Generation.

Before diving into the Prophecies that are the subject of this book, I want to bring up and mention the '*Dazzling Glory of God*'. This is described in the Jewish Bible, by God's Jewish Prophets to whom HE talked, and to whom HE provided Visions of Events HE saw taking place in a distant future.

It's an extraordinary experience '*to be able to see God*' - as His Prophets saw and described Him. There exists no 'superlative' powerful enough to describe the '*Dazzling Looks of God*', as especially His Prophet John from Patmos described Him in the book of Revelation 4:1-6, it's incredible – nothing like it ever seen. It's a must to read his description of Him. God is also described to some extent by Ezekiel in the Jewish Bible. They are the two Prophets who describe Him the best.

From those narratives, it's evident – that nobody can resemble His Glorious Looks in any way. I ask, how could anybody looking like God has been described, become a human being?

I recommend that especially people, who don't believe that God exists, take time to read what's written in the above passages!

Once we accept that God exists, we should ask ourselves, "Why do I exist?" and, "What is the purpose of my life?" In the Qur'an God reveals that our life here on earth is intended to prepare ourselves for our life in the hereafter. It's amazing, isn't it?

Where shall we look to find God? Turn inside and listen, and allow '*your little voice*' to talk to you. Generally, however, the lives we live have taken us away from God, why '**the little voice**' within has become silent. I say, whatever you are doing 'Stop' and turn to God asking Him to guide you; thanking Him for everything (in your heart).

One of the intentions of this book is – that it be of help to you to find your '*Innermost Being*' – *and thereby God*, hopefully creating '*consciousness*' in the minds of at least some of some people about the need to change our lives – not in some future, but now!

In a short time, things around us will begin to change, because the time to the end has become extremely short!

It's of fundamental importance to understand that the TORAH in the Hebrew Bible was the 'LAW' of God. The Jewish Bible was adopted into the Christian Bible and named '*The Old Testament*'.

To most people – who, as I see it really don't care - most of it seems like a jumble of '*Old Stories*' without importance of times long past. This includes most probably many of the Jews of today, and most, if not all Christians, Muslims, and peoples of pagan religions and Atheists.

In those '*Old Stories*' in the TORAH, the LORD God provided **His Ten Commandments** for the first time (Exodus 20 and Deuteronomy 5). Therein God provided His RULES for how we all (every human being) must worship only Him to be accepted into His Heavenly Kingdom! No unbelievers or pagans are accepted.

Intermingled into the stories of the Jewish people and their struggles, we find many Prophecies or Revelations of occurrences to come. Therein, Almighty God foretold and warned about terrible occurrences to affect our planet in a distant future.

From the many 'Signs' around us, it's evident that what HE warned about, the final and definitive eradication of mankind – no more to exist on Planet Earth, is upon us now.

God, the Almighty Creator, gave the TORAH, 'His LAW' to the Prophet Moses in the fourteenth-thirteenth century BC. The first and most important reason for this was 'to establish His LAW' under which the Jews (and every living human being – even if few people believe it) were (are) required to live. The TORAH contains the five Books of Moses – that are the first books in the Christian so-called Old Testament.

Genesis, the Book of 'The Origin' or 'Beginning', is the first Book in the TORAH and in the Christian Old Testament, wherein God for the first time revealed His creation of Adam, and thereby of mankind, Adam's offspring.

Providing the story of the Creation of Adam was of fundamental importance, to alert and warn mankind of an evil danger to learn to protect us against it.

But, as we've learned from 'Words of God' pronounced through the Prophet Jeremiah, one of the four Latter Prophets, fundamental God-given revelations, were eradicated from the TORAH by who God called "dishonest scribes" (different Bibles express this in different ways); something that is of sinister consequence to the destiny, not only to His Jewish people but for mankind, as a whole.

Because of the complexity of the subject of Prophecies - I've found that the way to introduce 'the theme' – is using passages of Prophecies (the Messages that God gave) from the Books of the Prophets Jeremiah, Isaiah, and Zephaniah in the Jewish Bible.

Why these Prophets? It's because they were the Spokespeople, Messengers, and Warners of God - warning of a future disastrous destiny for mankind. We need to understand that the End – our Destiny – has been caused purely by man - not by God.

Isaiah often named 'the Prince of Prophets' was the first of the so-called 'Latter Prophets' to whom – as I've found - God gave the most complete set of 'Messages' of any, to forewarn about why and how the End would (will) occur.

A vital matter obviously, is to '*Understand*' what is being described, because as mentioned, the way how the Prophets described things, was by writing '*what they thought they had seen in the Visions, they were given*'. But as we have learned the Prophets were unable to properly describe '*the factual true-life matters that God presented to them in His Visions*' that was what HE had seen taking place 'before His eyes'!

All Prophetic Revelations to the Prophets, Scriptural as well as non-Scripture, originated purely from God. What that means is that it's nothing any human being, can put our hands on.

We must believe in God and His Commandments, and worship Him with our hearts. HE has made it clear that it's to our personal detriment not to do it. To God, it makes no difference what we do, but it surely pleases Him when some of us choose His Way.

God's purpose with the Prophecies was, as we learn, to forewarn His Chosen Jewish people – but also mankind - about something (gruesome) that was to take place in some distant future. In doing so, God was giving an opportunity so to say, for us to '*take action*' to change the destiny we have been creating for ourselves; something, however, nobody ever '*understood*'.

I will continue by providing a series of Prophecies or revelations of God that HE initially entrusted to His two 'Latter Prophets' Jeremiah and Isaiah to pronounce. Later on, HE brings in Zephaniah and Malachi (the last of the Jewish Prophets two of the so-called 'Minor' Prophets).

The word 'Minor' only means, as indicated that the Book of the Prophet is very brief or short. Not that the Prophet and the Prophecies given through him were of minor importance.

In the Qur'an 3:187 it's written that when God made the Covenant with those to who (His Jewish Chosen People) HE gave the Book (the TORAH) HE told them, "*Spread the teachings of the Book (the TORAH) to mankind and do not conceal it; but they didn't pay attention to what God told them.*" (Not obeying what God had ordered them to do, keeping the knowledge for them, away from mankind)".

# 1.5 THE ONLY LIVING GOD COMMANDS OBEDIENCE TO HIM ALONE

Who is God? Does HE exist? I say it's of the essence that we change our conventional ways of how we think about God to re-shape our Beliefs. *HE is the Only Living God, the Creator and Owner of everything, who has existed from the beginning of time.*

Many or most people don't believe in the existence of God, the Only God that Exists – the Creator of everything. I ask - if God doesn't exist - how to explain the existence of His countless Prophecies – warning us about the future of our planet?

It may be hard to believe in any of this? But God the Creator of All gave us a '*Free Will*' to decide what we want to believe in! Therefore, don't blame Him for your wrong choices! Unfortunately, most of us – '*pick the broad evil way that belongs to Satan*' – which irreversibly takes us to '*Eternal perdition*'.

As indicated above, in addition to my desire to create 'Awareness' and 'Consciousness' of what's going on with our Planet Earth, a mayor Purpose of this Book is to help you to learn and understand that God, Who is the Only Living God Almighty Creator and Owner of Everything, Exists! I repeat this, because it's of fundamental importance to know!

People who don't believe in God, have their minds messed up by Satan, by giving them ideas of a multiplicity of inexistent (pagan) gods to worship. When this occurs, '*the little voice within*' is no longer heard. Those people can only hear the deceiving 'promises' of Satan that take away so many from '*the Narrow Way of God*'. Pay attention and know what you do!

Through the Prophet Isaiah 43:10-13, God makes it clear that 'HE is the Only Living God that exists and that there never was another god'. HE also said there will never be any other god.'

In Isaiah 44:6, God reaffirms that there is no other god beside Him.

The Commandments of the Only Living God are valid today, as when HE gave them to Moses some Three-Thousand-four-hundred years ago. They are valid for every human being, no exception made!

In Qur'an 2:57 HE tells the Jewish People that despite that HE gave their forefathers favors ahead of all peoples, they violated His Commandments. By violating His Commandments – HE says - *they didn't cause harm to Him, but they harmed their own souls.* This is what happens to everybody who violates the Commandments of God.

I want you to open your mind and think. God makes it clear that HE Created everything. HE is therefore the rightful owner of it all. This being the case, why would HE - Who possesses Powers beyond belief - want to share His Creation with anybody?

Having this in mind, the question we need to pose is how could God be challenged by any other being? And, from where would such being come?

The answer is there isn't anybody who can challenge God. The answer is also that Satan continuously provides deceiving ideas of god's who he has invented and whispers into the minds of '*listening religious leaders*'. Without 'understanding' what they were (are) doing, they helped Satan to take mankind away from '*The Narrow Way of God*' to 'eternal perdition', as 'inmates of Hellfire, as HE has established in Qur'an 2.39.

# 1.6 GOD'S COMMANDMENTS APPLY EQUALLY TO EVERY HUMAN BEING

In spite of what's mentioned in the foregoing, I want to pose the question relative to if God's ancient Commandments still are valid and for who? To respond to this, we *need to read God's First and subsequent Commandments, which* are to be viewed as the Pillar of His LAW – the TORAH - which HE gave to His Prophet Moses (read Exodus 20 and Deuteronomy 5), to be followed not only by His Jewish chosen people, but by every human individual.

In His Commandments, God defined His LAW for what HE Demands from every human individual in the Worship of Him to enable us to enter HIS HEAVENLY KINGDOM. One misstep and we are 'out of play'.

**THE MOST IMPORTANT COMMANDMENT OF GOD
as HE gave it to Moses. HE said,
I Am the LORD your God... , Worship No god but ME...**

You – and probably mostly everybody says, *"But, God gave His Commandments to Moses for the Jewish people, so they were (only) intended for them."*

It's true that God gave them to the Jewish people, but God made it clear that HE is the Only Living God (in the whole Universe), so His Commandments apply equally for every human being.

Individuals who don't strictly adhere to the Commandments of God – independently of what they think – the ones who HE calls 'unbelievers' 'pagans', are Not one of God's people!

God Commands every individual to seek Him (with faith and to believe in Him and worship only Him – in your heart; obeying His Commandments and LAW, as HE told His Prophet Moses.

Through His Prophet Isaiah God made it clear 29:13-14 that words – without involving the heart in the worship of Him aren't enough. He also indicates that only His Rules and Laws are valid; no man-made religious creeds, dogmas, doctrines, et al, are valid to Him.

Through Isaiah 29:10-11, God taught that the Prophets should be the eyes of the people, but that because of how they behaved, HE blindfolded them. They wouldn't be able to understand anything HE showed them in Visions.

Thereby, the meaning of His Prophetic Visions of our future was to be kept hidden from His Prophets (and from everybody else); it became as a sealed scroll until reaching the End.

From this we learn, why the Prophets weren't able to understand the Visions that God gave to them. This also gives the idea of why today nobody – including 'Earth-Scientists' - accept the Prophecies of God, wherein HE warned of future destructive occurrences that would affect Planet Earth.

As mentioned in the Introduction, God, the Almighty Creator and Owner of All, gave man a '*free will*', leaving it up to each one of us to do what we please, independently of if it's 'acceptable' to God or not. Nobody understands what we do to ourselves, when we do the wrong things that from the perspective of God are 'wicked'.

In the end, God doesn't care about what we do, but we, each one of us should, for the sake of our own 'Highest Good', because the salvation of each one of us can be attained only through God.

The majority of mankind in all probability thinks that they are 'doing well with God', but are they?

Through Jeremiah 8:11, what God indicated that the priesthood say that everything is well, when it is not, says it all!

Satan, the deceiver, whispers ideas in the minds of people, making them think that '*everything is well* ', when it isn't; after that he has deviated them away from '*the path of God* '.

It's imperatively important to understand that we must change our ways of being; in the knowledge that - as Jesus taught – to be accepted by God, to enter into His Kingdom is as hard as getting through a 'Needle's Eye', not just for the rich, but for everybody. In other words, it's just about impossible.

## 1.7 THE BECOMING OF THE QUR'AN (AL-QUR'AN)

Why was the Qur'an instituted? Even if it isn't mentioned directly anywhere – as far as I know - it came to be as the result - as mentioned before - of what God said through His prophet Jeremiah, 'My *LAW (the TORAH) has been changed*!' In other words, His LAW had been corrupted and had to be replaced!

We need to know – and this is critically important to have in mind - that God himself is the Author of the Qur'an. As far as I know, no other book has been authored by Him. HE authored the Qur'an **the Most Important Book** that has ever been published, to serve as '*The Guidance of Mankind*' for all of us without exception.

Translations of the Original Al-Qur'an from the original Arabic language, are viewed as '*the meaning*' of the Qur'an.

The reason to say this is because it's impossible to make exact translations of the Arabic texts to other languages.

I believe that my in-depth knowledge and understanding of the countless revelations in the Jewish Bible, wherein God 'talked to His Prophets', gives me the advantage to get 'the meaning' of the often (as I've learned) 'imperfect' translations to English.

I became curious about the Qur'an, not because somebody told me to read it, or because of an interest in Islam.

It was because I wanted to find out if there was any mention of the creation of Adam (of man) that's touched upon briefly in the Jewish Bible. If there was any such mention, I wanted to know what spiritual gifts God gave Adam when HE blew life into his nose thrills.

I was in for many surprises! The first – as mentioned - was learning that God was the Author of the Qur'an. The next major surprise was that God (Allah in Arabic) dedicates a significant amount of space in the Qur'an to talk about Adam and the circumstances around him at the creation.

I began to read and became more and more drawn into the Book to learn. It was remarkable to find an abundance of information about Adam, against the background that there's just nothing said about him in the Jewish Bible.

Where does the Qur'an fit in? Being the case, that God declared that the TORAH, His LAW, was 'corrupted' (Jeremiah 8:8) my understanding is that God authored the Qur'an for it to become **His Valid LAW** and the guiding principle for mankind. In other words, it wasn't intended solely for the Muslims - the people of Islam - but for mankind to learn from, independently of beliefs!

I discovered that the ancient Prophecies (Revelations of God) and stories in the Jewish Bible become far more *'understandable'* when compared with revelations made by God in the Qur'an. But, as certain texts in the Bible indicate, one must receive *'wisdom'* to attain the needed *'understanding'* of God's revelations.

My most significant finding, to which I'll return, and there's not the slightest doubt about it, is that it was the corrupted texts in the Jewish Bible and later in the Christian Bible that caused God to author the Qur'an (Al-Qur'an).

The texts of which I want to call "God's Heavenly Manuscript" were transferred verbally from God by His archangel Gabriel - to God's Prophet Mohammad. Mohammad was illiterate and could therefore not have written any of it. God chose him because of his great honesty.

I was a Christian for most of my life and know the New Testament quite well. But I find it most surprising that while God is present everywhere in the Qur'an, making 'countless' revelations, HE doesn't appear or make even one Revelation throughout the whole New Testament. Something to think about!

# 1.8 GOD WARNED AGAINST MAKING LIFE ON EARTH *'A PASTIME'*

Using one's personal wealth to live in material vain, ostentatious, conceited, pretentious circumstances - the home wherein you live, your elegant car and everything you surround yourself with - are signs of the need to 'show-off', of Ego.

It shows you are a self-important individual, something that must be avoided at any price, even to the point of giving away your wealth specifically to help the needy. Why is this you ask? It is because God is against man's greed and Narcissism (vanity, self-importance, egotism, selfishness, conceit, etc.).

I did at first not understand what God was saying in this revelation. But as I penetrated deeper and deeper into the teachings of God in the Qur'an, it began to dawn on me that God was warning us *not to treat our lives – while here on earth – 'as a mere pastime' – which doesn't serve a purpose*. Why was that, I wondered? Well, I mentioned it at the end of my introduction.

So, you ask, what is so important about this? I say, the problem I observe is that many or most people don't seem to believe there's a life after death, which is a serious mistake.

Today, there's so much evidence that our souls continue to live after the death of our bodies. Many people don't believe that there's a *'continuation of life'* after we finish our life here on earth, and that we go on to live in what God calls the *'Hereafter'*, which will continue for all eternity.

I have in my bookstand a book I bought some twenty-five years ago, titled *'Life after Life'*, authored by Doctor Raymond Moody MD, a psychiatrist who began to interview so-called near-death Patients, who against all the odds had *'come back to life'*. They 'came *back to life'* far beyond what's considered doable without getting brain damage, but quite remarkably none of them had suffered damage.

In talking with the *'revived'* patients, Moody learned of extraordinary experiences. They told him that when they died, the soul separated from the body, above which they floated for some time.

They could see everything that was going on around the body with doctors and nurses trying their best to revive the motionless body. Most of the souls were drawn into a tunnel of bright light and entered an environment - so peaceful - that they didn't want to leave. They were told they must return to the body for different reasons, but all were told they weren't ready yet.

Doctor Moody found that several out-of-body experiences had been dreadful. Those souls were taken to places in hellish environments where a multitude of people looked to be in horrible suffering. Those patients told Moody that their experiences had taught them a serious lesson that affected them deeply. They realized that they had been bad people and regretted how they had behaved against other people and how they had lived their lives.

I say they were very fortunate to be able to avoid the 'Day of Regret'. Moody learned that all those people underwent radical transformations for the better. Reading the book made me make adjustments *to make me a better me*.

Now back to what I've found to be warnings of God in the Qur'an that's directly related to the above heading, and also to the next sub-chapter *The Day of Regret*.

I narrate the interviews of Doctor Moody because they provide *vivid learning examples* - to learn from that Yes there's a Life after death. Where You will go, up or down, will depend on You!

Those who don't care, will deeply regret not having learned and done good deeds, accounted for in the respective individual 'Book of Deeds', the rewards for which will be enjoyed in the next life.

In Qur'an 3:14 and 18:46, we learn that 'Man is easily distracted in his brief worldly transitory life by material belongings, by wealth and by women and children (and much more).

But what is best, are good deeds, the effects of which will last forever and be rewarded by God in the Hereafter, as deserved!

In Qur'an 6:32, we learn that, *'Man extensively spends life on earth in play and having fun.'* This doesn't do us any good to enable us to get a good home, which only the believers (who believe in God) will get in the Hereafter.'

Qur'an 16:96, we learn, 'Whatever is with man in this earthly life is transitory, while what is with God will last forever. God will reward those who are patient according to the best of their deeds.'

God, the Almighty Creator, is All-Knowing, All-Seeing, All-Wise, All-Aware. Because God is All-Knowing, HE knows that the vast Majority of mankind will deeply regret what they didn't strive for while here on earth, to make themselves to deserve a good place in the Hereafter, in His everlasting Kingdom!

It's well worth your while to learn from the following sub-chapter 1.12 about what God calls "*The Day of Regret*" in the Qur'an.

## 1.9 ' *THE DAY OF REGRET* ' - WHEN IT WILL BE TOO LATE

I believe that even if God doesn't mention it anywhere, HE maybe feels sorry for all people, the vast majority, who will go to hell. Why? After reading the Qur'an many times to learn from God's teachings, I found that HE time after time mentioned what HE calls '*The Day of Regret*' and even *'The Day of Intense Regret*'; better known as 'The Day of Resurrection, immediately followed by '*Judgment Day*'. It is the Day when we all, both the living and the dead who will be resurrected, will be brought to trial in front of '**The Just Judge**'.

In the following, I provide a few mentions of God in the Qur'an, related to what HE calls '*the Day of Regret*'. The excerpts from the Qur'an and the non-Qur'an verses at the end provide 'Food for Thought' related to how we need to change our lives!

In Qur'an 2:167 we learn that the unbelievers shall say that if there was a way for them to return, then they would renounce those who made them to sin. God will show them *what they did wrong, which will be of intense regret to them*, but they shall not be able to escape from the Fire.'

Qur'an 3:156. Those of you, who believe, don't become like those who disbelieve. To them, God will make it to be '*an intense regret*' in *their hearts*. HE is the giver of life and causes death. HE is All-Knowing, All-Wise and sees all that we do.

## 1.10 ABOUT INTERCESSION - GOD SAID - *"ONLY I CAN FORGIVE"*

The Roman Catholic Church established that they can forgive the Sins of their Catholic followers. According to the teachings of the Catholic Church Jesus was an '*Offer Lamb*' who – through his sufferings and crucifixion - washed away what they call the '*Original Sin*' of mankind committed by Adam and Eve.

But, as we learn from what God teaches in the Qur'an, HE forgave Adam and Eve; therefore, there was no sin left that needed to be washed away. Wherefrom did the Roman Catholic Church get the idea of the 'Original Sin', and of an 'Offer Lamb' – Jesus - who washed it away? It seems to be that Satan has the answer. It was yet another of his amazing strokes of a genius.

In numerous passages in the Qur'an, God has revealed that **Nobody** (priests, Jesus, the Virgin Mary, saints, angels, prophets, any other) can intercede for anybody – only HE can forgive. Consequently, this is a matter of great contention. Please refer to the Qur'an, Chapters 2: [47-48], 2: [122-123], 2:[255], 3: [128-129], 6:70, 32:4. 39:[43-44]. The following sentences will give you something to think about!

Qur'an 2:255 teaches that there is no God but HE, the Living, the Eternal; Who can intercede for anybody, who can forgive.

Qur'an 32:4, There's no Intercessor besides Him.

Qur'an 3:128-129, Nobody has authority to intercede. It's exclusively upon God whether He forgives or punishes whom He pleases.

Qur'an 39:43-44, Unto God belongs all intercession! HE is the Supreme Ruler and Owner of the heavens and the earth.

As we learn from the above, the matter of intercession belongs exclusively to God. No one else can intercede to forgive!

Whoever acts pretending to have the right (that he doesn't have) to forgive sin - commits a heinous offense against God that will be punished; it creates a situation for the Catholic 'forgiven ones', who have been made to believe that they are forgiven their offences against God - which it's apparent they aren't. But they walk around in that belief.

After learning this, the question to ask the Catholic Church is, 'who gave them authority to intercede for God to forgive sins?'

# 1.11 TROUGH JEREMIAH GOD SAID *"MY LAW HAS BEEN CHANGED"*

What we deal with here is the TORAH in the Jewish Bible, which God called His LAW, of which HE said through His Prophet Jeremiah "My LAW *has been changed* ".

Although Isaiah was the first of God's so-called 'latter Prophets' - a Messenger - I'll begin with Jeremiah, another of His important so-called Latter Prophets, and go on with Isaiah.

Jeremiah lived in the latter part of the seventh century and the first part of the sixth century BC. Through Jeremiah, the LORD God pronounced what is – as I've found - besides His Ten Commandments, on of His *'His most astounding revelations'* in the Jewish Bible (the Christian Old Testament) as we shall learn.

In Jeremiah 8:4-6, God speaks through him addressing His Jewish people. We learn that HE is upset with them because they don't seek or worship Him, and prefer to worship idols instead of Him. HE rebuts them for not turning to Him and not being sorry, but kept going their way, getting lost.

In Jeremiah 8:7-9 and 12 HE told them they didn't know the rules by which HE ruled them. HE questions their knowledge and wisdom about His Laws (The TORAH) *when HE told them that His Law had been changed by them.* (Different Bibles present this in different ways, but God's message is clear).

Jeremiah told the Jewish people that their wise men were put to shame, because they were confused. He went on telling them that (in doing what they had done, by changing and deleting His Words in His LAW, the TORAH) by rejecting His words they were lost leaving them without wisdom (needed to understand) that's given by God.

Since nobody has known what was *'wronged'* - the Jewish Bible was never corrected. What was said by God is valid today for the Jewish People and every human being, same as when God pronounced His Words. And, His Words – which are eternal everlasting - prevail over words of any human being.

From the revelations of God, we learn the troubling fact that some parts of His LAW the TORAH – (the books of Moses in the Jewish Bible, Old Testament) *were changed by the Jewish Priesthood.*

It's a shocking revelation on the part of God (unchanged until this day) that HE told His Jewish People through Jeremiah.

It's the only place in the Jewish Bible where this matter is brought up. But God also brings it up in the Qur'an, and the only One who could know this fact, to write it therein, is God.

How many scholars have paid attention to this most significant revelation – of major consequence - not only to the Jewish People but to mankind as a whole? It's of vital importance to understand that the LAWS of God (His Commandments – and very especially His First and adjoining Commandments, the ones that Christianity disapproved of and rejected, as we learn in the New Testament) apply the same to all mankind – independently of religions that have been defined by human rules (creeds or dogmas) which God doesn't accept, as indicated in 29:14.

In Qur'an 21:92 God said that the Ummah (The Islamic religion) HE put in place through His Prophet Mohammad, is one and HE is our God, therefore worship only Him.

Changing the Words of God in the TORAH - His LAW – or anywhere is a no-no that comes with the highest price that will be paid when we move to the next life, to the Hereafter.

Through Jeremiah 23:23-24, God also said, that HE is a God who is everywhere and not in one place only. Nobody can hide where HE can't see him.

In the Qur'an God says that HE is everywhere in heaven and on earth. Thus, God is everywhere, Omniscient, Omnipresent and Omnipotent. HE sees and knows everything. Nobody can hide from Him.

There isn't the shade of a doubt, as I see it that in the Qur'an (Al-Qur'an) God brought *back to life* texts that HE must have given to Moses, which one way or the other became eradicated from the TORAH, probably I believe, when the Jewish Bible became printed.

With His many detailed revelations in the Qur'an God told mankind about Satan, to uncover who he is.

Why it is important to know about Satan, is to enable us to protect ourselves against him; the Terrible Enemy and Nemesis of man – who has dedicated himself full time, to bring mankind to fall away from '*the Way of God*'. And, indeed, most have fallen.

My narrative that follows a '*timeline*' given in the *Abrahamic Scriptures* (Jewish Bible and Qur'an), provides insights of what one may call '*the Spiritual History of Mankind*' – from the beginning to the end – and '*Why*' and '*How*' '*our end*' *is destined to happen*' - and, even approximately '*When*' it's going to occur.

Through His numerous Prophecies, God gave '*His Chosen People*' many chances '*to wake up* ' – to try to understand that a radical and profound change was/is needed in their ways of being; that is valid, now even more then when HE issued His warnings.

When we look around us, it's evident from the sinister occurrences that are taking place around our planet - that evil dominates our world.

The most important missing (eradicated) text of all in the TORAH is doubtless when Adam and Eve asked God to forgive them for having disobeyed Him – which God revealed in the Qur'an that HE did. I'll return to this matter of great importance in Chapter 2.

At issue is that Religious Leaders lack the ' *understanding* ' that quite a few of God's Revelations that for sure must have given to Moses, were left out when the Jewish Bible became printed. It was - I believe - one of the things that infuriated God making him '*furiously angry* ', as HE revealed through His Prophet Isaiah - who comes next.

In Qur'an 6:91 it's written, that they - the Jewish People - did not estimate God, as they should have, when they said that HE did not send down anything to any human being. In other words, the revelations God gave to His Prophet Moses in the TORAH – His LAW – valid for every human being, including you, me and everybody!

## 1.12 GOD REVEALS HIS ANGER AGAINST MANKIND, THROUGH ISAIAH

I want to underline that the 'End-of-Time' Prophecies that God revealed through His Prophet Isaiah - the first of several of God's so-called 'Latter Prophets' – are amongst the most dreadful of all. God's ancient Prophecies are of *'Monumental Consequence'* to mankind. The most important revelations were about *'His furious anger against not only His Chosen People, but against all mankind'*.

The splitting over time of Judaism in different, so-called *'denominations' or 'sects'* has been of great consequence. The most important is that the liturgy *'departs from the original strict liturgy' that God established through Moses and his brother Aaron.*

Therein God defined how HE must be worshipped. HE was (is) so strict that when two of Aaron's sons (priests) disobeyed God inside the tent where 'the Covenant Box' was kept, the two were instantly punished and killed.

Through His last Prophet (in the Jewish Bible) Malachi 4:4 God said that the Jewish people needed to *be mindful of the teachings HE gave to Moses, to whom HE gave the Laws, and Rules at Mount Sinai for the people of Israel,* which obviously included the liturgy. Elsewhere, God has indicated that His Laws apply equally for all mankind.

There are other reasons as well, to which I shall return. Not taking into account God's 'End-of-Time' revelations is a mistake with colossal ramifications that's on the way to cost mankind dearly, as we shall learn.

Isaiah, God's foremost Latter Prophet (Spokesperson or Messenger), lived close to two thousand eight hundred years ago, about five hundred and some years after Moses. Isaiah was the first Prophet through who Almighty God pronounced Revelations wherein HE specifically addressed matters to occur at the 'End-of-Time', which foretold future occurrences of grave consequence to mankind. All of it, to take place in a distant future!

Isaiah wrote as God told him. Some of what he wrote, unimportant today, was related to occurrences that took place at his time. God's important revelations from the perspective of mankind today – were all related to a distant future – the one that doubtless has arrived, '*knocking at our doors*'. Those revelations are remarkable because God provided visions of how Planet Earth – rather its atmosphere - would be affected and what would happen to our planet.

Herein are some of the Prophesied occurrences:

Isaiah 2:14 and 16. God *will crush the highest Mountains.* HE *will sink even the largest ships.* This sounds as the result of Tidal or Rouge waves coming into motion.

Isaiah 9:19. God is angry why His punishment will burn like fire through the countries and destroy the people.

Isaiah 13:5 and 9. Because God is angry, HE will devastate the whole earth.

Isaiah 13:10. The sun will be dark. (This in all probability to be caused by black volcanic ashes filling the skies, resulting from the effects of the Global Warming.)

If you have followed what's going on with our planet on the Internet, I'm sure you have observed there's an increased activity of volcanoes coming to life spewing out ashes and smoke, like the Volcano Stromboli in Italy (August 27, 2019), and so many more.

Isaiah 13:13. God said that HE will make the heavens tremble, and the earth to be shaken out of its place on the Day when HE will show His anger.

This is an exceptional revelation because it sounds as if our planet is going to be departing from its current Orbit, on the Day when it collapses, when our time is up.

Very curiously, Merlin (sub-chapter 7.4) said that the Planets of our Solar System would abandon their orbits.

Through Isaiah 24:1-6 we learn that *God has pronounced a curse on the Earth.* We also learn that mankind is going to pay a high penalty for its transgressions (evil doings).

There exists an array of revelations of catastrophe foretold by God through Isaiah and several newer Prophets of God (among them Jesus).

Similar revelations have been pronounced over and over, as well in the Qur'an (Established close to fourteen-hundred years later and what a coincidence, about fourteen-hundred years ago).

Isaiah 24:19. God said that the earth's foundations will tremble. The earth will crack and shatter and split open (when the Tectonic Plates break apart). The earth will collapse (overturn) and never rise again (Be as we know it today).

What God revealed in Isaiah 24:23 that 'the sun will no longer shine...' was repeated in later revelations. It, no doubt, will be caused by countless Volcano eruptions all over our planet, darkening the skies, and maybe also by the Yellowstone Super Volcano, which Scientists think is getting ready to erupt.

These terrible revelations of God have many things going that were repeated many times by later Prophets both in the Bible and in the Qur'an. But, what's the meaning of it all, including the mentions of the stars that Isaiah described as 'falling like figs in a strong wind'? The explanation to this occurrence is provided in sub-Chapter 8.13.

Are those terrible Prophesies still valid? What did His 'Chosen People' and mankind do to make God so upset and furiously angry?

God was (is) upset with the Jewish People for their lack of attention to Him, 'their Benefactor' who had preferred them – the offspring of Jacob – the son of Isaac and grandson of Abraham - among all peoples.

The Words of God, through Isaiah, are alarming and were surely meant to get His chosen people, to think about the reasons (why HE pronounced them) and consequences of His Words – that reveal His fury building up against His Chosen People and doubtless against mankind.

Mankind - all of us – including you and me - must obey the LAWS and Commandments that 'the only Living God' gave to His Prophet Moses and also in the Qur'an to His Prophet Mohammad, which are valid for every living human being.

Man-made laws or rules defining a religion are unacceptable to God, as HE revealed in Isaiah 29:13-14, as descried before.

How could all of this have happened? The answer is that our unseen Nemesis, Satan, has made sure that the great majority of mankind *fall into his cleverly disguised traps of deceit* – destined to go to the fires of Hell.

All of those, who don't believe in God, or who are in doubt, what do you say about all these revelations? Did you pay attention to what is (was) being said? Are they simply words?

On the Day of Regret all *wrongdoers* will know you were wrong; and there will be no way back. Satan will stand at the entrance to Hell welcoming you, saying something like, *"Welcome to my flames, have a gruesome scorching stay for all eternity"*! Well, on second thought, he will have thousands of his devils welcoming all '*wrongdoers*' at the gates of Hell.

Kind of something to think about, for those who don't realize that we – everyone of us - have been given a purpose for our lives, and for all the wicked people and don't care about anything, who don't have respect for others!

Don't you think it's time to stop what you are doing and begin to reflect upon '*the Purpose of your Life*'!

I want again to call the attention to the fact that the Words of God – especially His Ten Commandments - are as valid Today, as when HE uttered them.

Today, when I write this, is June the 21st, 2018. The reason to mention a date is that today an article was published that was on the first page on News papers around the world that reads: *"Israeli Prime Minister's wife, charged with fraud, breach of trust."*

The Article continues mention that the PM himself, Mr. Netanyahu, is under Police Investigation for abuse of Power. I say, how sad! I doubt God approves of any of that, which has to do with anybody taking advantage of people for his own benefit.

Well, as we know, the wife had to go to court and Mr. Netanyahu has been accused of improper doings, which I'm sure isn't approved.

# 1.13 GOD REVEALS HIS FURIOUS ANGER THROUGH ZEPHANIAH

It took some time before I got to the Book of the Prophet Zephaniah from around 620 B.C., a Prophet I had never heard of.

The Book is just a few pages, so it's very short. But what God told Zephaniah, His Messages, which are '*to the point*', are appalling, because God defines that HE is addressing all of mankind not just His so-called 'Chosen People'. There's no way of misunderstanding what HE says.

Through Zephaniah 1:2-3, the LORD declared that HE will destroy everything on planet earth, man and beast, the birds in the sky, and the fish of the seas.

HE says HE will destroy mankind bringing the downfall of the wicked (who, God destined to go to Hell, according to His revelations in the Qur'an). It's impossible not to understand what God said in this revelation. It's distinct - to the point!

In Zephaniah 1:17, God said that HE will bring terrible disasters on the people, because they sinned against Him. Their dead bodies will be rotting on the ground.

This sounds similar to the terrible revelations of John from Patmos wherein are described different forms of punishment – supernatural in nature – that will eradicate mankind.

Through Zephaniah 1:18 it's said 'On the day when the LORD shows His fury, all their wealth shall not benefit them to save themselves. The whole earth will be destroyed by the fire of the wrath of God (erasing all live, human, as well as animal.'

Through Zephaniah 3:8 God said, that when HE will gather nations together to pour out His annoyance upon them, all the earth shall be consumed by the fire of His anger.

After reading this, is there any doubt of the unfortunate destiny whereto we're headed? And, mind you, the time left has become very short?

The question to be made is. How come Christian priests and preachers never bring up these revelations of God, and so, provide the

Truth? Even if it now is far too late to change our destiny – what man has built; we, every individual, need to understand and be conscious of what God has said.

We need to change the sumptuous opulent ways of living of so many of us, before it's too late.

It's evident that there's no Benevolent God, but that God, the One and Only God is 'furiously angry' with mostly All of us!

The overwhelming issue is - time. Will it be later in the future or now? Based on my compilation of ancient and more recent Prophecies and on the situation of the Global Warming, I will show you that our end is now in our generation.

Every individual needs to take action and make his/her best, to appease God for his/her own sake, turning to Him – and only Him (as a voice told me when I was Six years of age; '*don't worship Jesus, worship God*') - in worship – asking Him in your hearts for forgiveness for your sins – asking for guidance. God will listen to you when you turn to Him in your heart!

## 1.14 BOOK OF REVELATION'S TERRIBLE END-OF-TIME PUNISHMENTS

This book early on called my attention. I want to say that I read it over and over again for years, without understanding its revelations; i.e., it's a strange mishmash of unrelated phrases, and terrifying messages of doom and destruction, until now.

In Spanish Bibles, John's Book of Revelation is often called '*El (the) Apocalypsis*', a word that originates from an ancient Greek word 'Apo-kalypsis', which means '*something uncovered*, which is *ultimately destined to go to hell*'.

It sounds scary and is something to which mankind ought to have paid attention, as it surely was God's intention when HE provided his dreadful Revelations of terrible sufferings. Early on I found that a great many of the writings in this book didn't make sense, why they undoubtedly must have been re-written.

John from Patmos was given '*previews*' of the End of the World (our Planet), to be total devastation, similar to what was foretold by God for the first time, through Isaiah – and later on by other Prophets. The question again is – why was that?

In this Book John tells us he saw God, providing extraordinary details of His aspects as follows.

Revelation 4:1-3, 5-6, (read it all – the Bible or Internet - because this is awesome) John wrote that he had another vision and that he saw an open door in heaven. A voice that sounded like a trumpet, which he had heard before, told him to come up to be shown what would happen. John describes how a Spirit took him up to heaven. I am quite sure that what took place must have been shown to John in a dream, because as God told to Moses, who asked to see Him, His Glory - the light that God emits - would have burnt him.

John says that he saw a throne with someone sitting on it. His face gleamed like precious stones. And around the Throne, there was a rainbow the color of an emerald.

What an extraordinary vision of God.

The text that continues in the Book of Revelation is important, but goes beyond the scope of this book – that is to bring out in the open what's going on in God's Prophecies.

I've found that the precondition to enable us to '*understand*' the Prophecies is to frequently '*worship God*' and 'to have faith and *believe in Him without doubt*', as HE requires and Commands in His Commandments. It's something I do several times every day, but no longer as a Christian, for reasons that will be clear, as you read this Book.

Most of us (mankind) have fallen away from God. Why is that? The most important reason is because people don't believe in God. And that will take to Hell those who don't believe in Him.

In Revelation 13:18, John declares that such a thing calls for wisdom. Whoever is intelligent (has the gift of 'understanding') can figure it out."

In Revelation 17:9, John declares, "*This calls for* (the need to have the gift of) *wisdom and understanding*" (that is, to understand the meaning of the Visions – he and other Prophets had been given about the terrible things to occur in some distant future.

It is our personal faith and belief – with the heart - in the only Living God that '*opens the gates of understanding of the mind' that allows us to receive 'wisdom and understanding*'; that is what will help us to find the way to God.

We need to understand that God accepts us 'on His, the only living God's terms alone'.

Mankind, without having the slightest idea of what it has done to itself – one can say - walked away from God; something HE doesn't care about because it doesn't affect Him, something that makes Satan happy.

I said that God doesn't care about it, but in a way, I believe HE does, because to those of us who strictly abide by His LAWS and Commandments – without straying away – there's the Promise of life in His Kingdom, that I deal with frequently throughout this Book, because my Friends, this is the singularly most important matter that we need to know about and take care off.

It is those who have become 'wrongdoers' HE doesn't care about, who are destined for Hell. I ask the 'believers', "are you sure you are a by God accepted 'believer'"?

In the Book of Revelation, God provides information, as warnings about the terrible punishments that HE will bestow to mankind for not believing in Him and strictly obeying His Commandments and worshipping Him, as HE demands – being that HE is the only Living God!

# 1.15 "NOBODY CAN HIDE WHERE I CANNOT SEE HIM," SAID GOD

Through Jeremiah 23:23-24 God declared that '*HE is a God who is near at hand - and not a God far away. If a man enters a hiding place, HE sees him.*'

In the Qur'an 22:70 it's said, '*Know that God knows all that is in the heaven and on the earth?*'

In these phrases God is alerting us that we need to know the fact that HE sees and knows everything we do and say, and even our thoughts. In other words, HE knows our actions - all of them – the good and the bad. Sadly, the vast majority of the actions of mankind are wrong and therefore unacceptable to God.

In Qur'an 82:11-12 God teaches that HE has placed a guardian angel with each one of us writing down in each individual's '*Book of Deeds*' everything that occurs it our lives, to be presented on Judgment Day.

God knows everything we do. HE knows that many or most human beings spend time and money to 'venerate' and 'idolatrize' human beings; such as sports or film or music 'stars' (idols), and so many others celebrating at Festivals, TV-shows and other Events.

HE who gave us life and everything else, knows that HE is rarely – if ever - in the minds and hearts of most human beings. HE knows that HE hardly ever is worshipped by us, as HE the Creator – and Owner of everything has Commanded!

HE knows that mostly all the revered star idols behave as if they were 'gods', especially the 'vein" who live sumptuous 'pastime' lives in overabundance and the 'greedy' who don't help the poor and the needy. It will cost them their salvation.

## 1.16 GOD CREATED MAN AS SPIRITUAL BEINGS (- A QUALITY LONG TIME LOST –) AND A PURPOSE

In reading the Story of the Creation of Adam in the Book of Genesis in the Bible, but especially in the Qur'an which is very detailed, we learn that God, the Almighty Creator, ongoing met in person with Adam and later on also with Eve in Paradise.

Because Adam and Eve could both see and speak with Him, we can conclude that they were spiritual beings, although not spirits or angels, since they had human bodies.

But, as we know, everything changed dramatically for them after they fell for the temptations of Satan, thereby disobeying and sinning against God. They immediately became aware of what they had done and were afraid.

God rebuked them harshly for having disobeyed Him; something that prompted Adam and Eve (according to revelations of God in the Qur'an) to ask Him for forgiveness for their sin, which God revealed that HE did. We shall look at all of that in Chapter 2 to find out what happened at God's creation of Adam, which God has revealed in detail in the Qur'an.

God forgave Adam and Eve their sin, but because they had disobeyed Him – despite that HE had warned them of Satan - God punished them, expelling them and (this is important) simultaneously also Satan from Paradise.

When it happened, Adam and Eve lost their privileges and mainly that of having an on-going contact with their Creator.

From that moment on they began to lose their 'inbuilt' spiritual qualities and abilities, the ones that God had given to Adam through His breath when HE blew life and a soul through his nostrils. In the Qur'an, we learn (as I see it) that God 'showed off' to His angels and the Jinn (another kind of being), regarding the mental capabilities to memorize, that HE had bestowed to Adam.

But, from then on, with God no more being near them, as HE had been while they were in Paradise, there wasn't anything that stimulated them (the progenitors of mankind) to use any of their unique God-given capabilities. As a result, those capabilities or aptitudes - something we, every human being '*have inbuilt in us*' – as I've discovered – became more and more '*dormant*'.

Only now and then will we find people (very few) who excel because they have been able to '*awaken*' and use, some of those God-given abilities, skills, and talents.

The lives of Adam and Eve from then on were spent in a constant struggle to survive in the harsh conditions outside of paradise. As I believe, God was somehow still somewhere around, but at a (spiritual) distance; a distance that over time became greater and greater.

It happened as the result of the continually diminishing spirituality of mankind, who God in the Qur'an calls '*the children of Adam*', (*Observe that God doesn't call them "My children"*) as the wickedness of mankind extended everywhere; as Satan made it '*to fall his way*', or as his probable parade song about mankind goes, "*They're falling My Way*".

When we read the Jewish Bible and the Qur'an – and reflect upon what's being said - it's evident - as I've learned - that God has nothing good to say about mankind as a whole (except those few who worship Him in their hearts and follow His Commandments).

On the other hand, HE has expressed His anger, fury and even His furious anger against mankind, who HE has said, HE will punish and exterminate.

One has to put forward the question that - given these circumstances - How will it be possible for anybody, who doesn't strictly follow God's Commandments to be admitted into His Kingdom?

It's of fundamental importance to understand that salvation isn't granted just because you go to Church, or the Synagogue, or the Mosque, or any temple (Buddhist or Hindu, or any other) and say ('*lip-service*') that you believe in God. Unless you believe in Him and only Him in your heart, strictly adhering to His Commandments, there will be no admittance to heaven!

Today exist about Seven and a half Billion inhabitants on our planet of which I say; only a few percent - will be allowed to enter the Kingdom of God. That's how successful Satan has been deviating man from the Narrow Way of God. Don't ask how I know; it is simply so.

In the Qur'an 102, God made the following revelation that's vital to have in mind. HE said that *the cause of man's (impending) destruction (and of Mother Earth) is mutual rivalry for worldly gains.* (Caused by 'egoism', 'selfishness', 'envy', 'greed' and … 'man's need for wealth, material belongings, and power to dominate our kin and our planet for selfish cravings to satisfy his ego).

What good is it to be rich and powerful? Well, while the rich and powerful are alive the few years they live here on earth they maybe enjoy it, although it's questionable. But the fundamental question that needs to be made is - and what about afterwards in the '*Hereafter*'?

I state that it's time to give deep thought to this matter.

What's so utterly mind-boggling is that you unknowing, Satan, your Nemesis, who is the Nemesis of mankind, has deceived you and mostly all human beings to '*fall away from God's way*', which means losing the chance to enter into the Kingdom of God.

By reading the Jewish Bible we find that God tried to guide His so-called '*Chosen people*' to learn to walk in His narrow Way which, as I believe, HE finally gave up doing, as they kept rebelling against Him.

I suggest you read and think (it's worth your while to do it) about what God said about the Jewish priests and prophets through His Prophet Jeremiah 6:14 and 8:11. '*All is well,* the priests said to the people, *when – as God said - all wasn't well…*' And, can you believe it, God repeated this short phrase numerous times.

In reading Jeremiah Chapter 8, we found that many things were very wrong between God and the Jewish people.

Why do I suggest reviewing what God said therein? I do, because I believe that most humans unconsciously may think (if at all) '*that all is well*', as God told His Jewish people about in this passage, while the reality is that '*all is as far away from being well for our planet and us;*' as this Book will show.

On Judgment Day God will ask "*What did you do with the life I gave you?*" What are you going to answer?

## 1.17 SIGNS THAT PORTEND THE ARRIVAL OF THE END

As mentioned, there are several Events or Signs - as I call them — that are in place or close to getting in place, affecting, or just about to affect our World (Planet Earth) one way or the other. They portend the imminence of the End of our Time, as prophesized. They are:

### 1. Prophecy of the 112 Last Popes.

This is the first Sign for the reason that it is in place. Bishop Malachi of Ireland Prophesized about 112 future Popes. (See Sub-Chapter 7.3 for details about Malachi (1094-1148) and his Prophecies). It's evident that there exist question-marks about the integrity of this Prophecy, and that - as some believe - it might be some kind of hoax. After reading it over and over, I've concluded that there is a high probability that it is true, the reason to bring it in. This is so because his Prophecies of especially the recent Popes have been exacting.

The 112th, and thus the last Pope in accordance to Malachi's list of Popes, is the current one, Francis. Per the same list, the last Pope was supposed to call himself 'Peter the Roman'.

Francis, the current 112th Pope in most certainty knew about the Prophecies of Malachi and probably thought he could evade his fate by choosing a different name, which was easy. But, how to avoid being the 112th Pope – the Last – on the list?

I say that being that the popes were numbered, the name as such becomes irrelevant - while being the 112th and thus the last Pope - pinpoints him exactly and tells us loud and clear that we are at the end of time.

At the End-of-Time during the time of the Last Pope, we learn in Revelation 14:8 '*Babylon, the Great City* (the Vatican), *has fallen...*' the church is to be destroyed during 'the great tribulation', which will last for forty-two Months.

### 2. Setting the Stage for a Prophesied Evil Ruler.

The place, as foretold, is the Middle East - where we have seen the overthrow of dictators. The insurrection in Syria that's led by its Sunni Muslim majority in opposition to a minority government of the tyrant

Assad, who belongs to a small sect of Alawite Muslims, an offspring of the Shiites. The revolt that began in 2011 is totally unpredictable. This is so because it's aggravating sectarian tensions (Sunni Vs Shiite) beyond its borders in a region shaken by severe religious, ethnic and political divisions – that took off after the American invasion of Iraq. It was an enormous mistake, because with Sadam Hussein out of the way, a Shiite Iran was free to support Assad in Syria, free of constraints!

The extraordinarily violent scenario in Syria – involving surrounding Countries, Israel, Lebanon and Turkey, as well as the USA, Russia and Iran, is – I believe - setting the stage for the appearance of a unique individual, as written in the Book of Daniel 11:21-22, wherein an angel told Daniel as follows:

The next Ruler will be an evil man who has no right to be king (Ruler) but will appear unexpectedly in Syria and seize power by trickery. Anyone opposing him, even God's high priest will be wiped out. By making treaties (with Russia and Iran), he will deceive many nations, and will grow stronger and stronger, even though this ruler only rules a small country.

In Daniel 9:27 we learn that the Ruler will have a firm agreement with many people for seven years. When half that time is past, he will put an end to sacrifices and offerings (to God).

That's when the great tribulation will begin, to last three and a half years – until the End. This goes well hand-in-hand with what's said in Revelation 13:7that follows.

The angel tells Daniel 7:25 that God's people will be under his power for three and a half years, after which the evil Ruler will be destroyed (by God).

In the Book of Revelation, we learn that 'a beast' will emerge. In Revelation 13:5 and 7 we learn that 'The beast will be allowed to make claims that will be insulting to God'.

We learn that the foretold evil Ruler will be permitted (by God) to have authority for forty-two months (the second half of the seven years) over every tribe, nation, language, and race. He will be allowed to fight against God's people and kill them.

Qur'an 27:82, God declares that HE shall bring out from the earth a beast to the unbelievers, which shall speak to them because mankind believed not in Him (God) and His revelations."

As we find, 'the beast' is mentioned both in the Qur'an and in the Book of Revelation. It will emerge at the end of time and will try to change the true religion.

I will return to the 'Ruler' and the 'beast' in Chapter 4.

### 3. Edgar Cayce's Amazing Prophecies of what he was given to 'see'

We need to understand that without God giving Cayce the 'powers' enabling him to 'see' our future, he wouldn't have been able to do it. I therefore believe that the Prophecies provided by Cayce, is the most overwhelming of all 'Signs' extensively because he lived in our time. Sometime in the 30s and early 40s, Cayce provided a series of revelations of devastation, which he said were to begin to happen in our time.

Detailed information about Cayce and what he what he was given to see in his horrifying visions is provided in Sub-Chapter 5.1.

### 4. The Effects of the man-made Global Warming on the Oceans.

This is, without a doubt – '*the element*' - that's 'ticking' (as a 'time-bomb') in the depths of the rapidly warming and un-evenly raising waters of the Oceans.

On the Internet we find mentions of the constant acceleration of the melting of the vast ice-sheets in Greenland, in Antarctica and elsewhere.

The resulting effect of the colossal ice loss acceleration in certain places translates into massive amounts of water being distributed throughout the Oceans. But the distribution is uneven, with some locations 'pulling' more water than other. And this phenomenon – that nobody ever discusses - is causing a growing imbalance to our planet that's changing its Dynamics and principally the Gravity, causing it to rapidly become more and more imbalanced, and its rotation to become more unstable.

And this is the 'element' as I called above that's driving Planet Earth towards devastation, to take place – not in a distant future – but very soon, in our Generation.

In chapter 8 you'll find detailed information of this contentious matter, putting in place evidence about how our planet will (is about to begin to) be devastated, thereby fulfilling the prophecies of God.

I want to repeat what I said before that this isn't something that God put in place for us. God saw what was going to happen to our planet in a remote future. And HE also saw what it was that would cause our devastation to take place.

It's the evil, egoistic, avaricious ways of behaviour of the great majority of mankind. Nobody ever listened to the oft-repeated warnings of God, so, nothing was ever done to change the 'Unfortunate Destiny' we have been constructing for our planet and ourselves.

Terribly for us, the very advanced state of ice-melt acceleration can't be reversed or stopped.

# 1.18 MIRACLES AND WONDERS OF NATURE OF A UNIQUE PLANET

**- something that human beings haven't recognized to be miracles -**

You surely ask, what's the meaning of this? It is that we humans take for granted that what we see around us is how it has to be. I say that imbedded in what we see are 'miracles' or 'wonders' of nature that God, the Creator of All, gave our planet aimed to make it enjoyable to our eyes and minds.

The fact that everything has a tendency to evolve as time passes, doesn't mean that what we see, progressed from one and the same molecule or mollusc. It was - and is - that God in his benevolence, kindness and generosity gave and gave and gave.

I want to begin with flowers and I continuously give thanks to God for the beautiful flowers I see, the large visible ones as well as the small almost microscopic ones of different kinds, shapes and colours that grow in my not at all well taken care of lawn.

It's precisely because it isn't well taken care of that I have that myriad of minuscule flowers that I see and enjoy; for which I give Him thanks. It so happens that when the lawns are perfect looking, they are that way because tons of herbicides were used to kill the weeds that carry the small wild-flowers.

The Bougainvillea, below, is my preferred flower that covers all the collars of the rainbow. Where I saw the most colours was in Brazil, between the Capital City of Brasilia and the airport.

Okay – that's in regards to flowers.

What about Birds? Did you know that there exist 338 species of hummingbirds (called Colibris in many other languages, such as in Spanish and in Swedish) worldwide, the tiniest of all birds. The smallest one measuring one and a half Inch in size. I saw one in El Salvador, in Central America, which I initially thought to be a bumble bee, until realizing it was a hummingbird.

One of so many Colibris.

What do you know about the Albatross? There are somewhat more than a dozen different species; to be found in the Southern Ocean and the Pacific Ocean. The largest of these seabirds can reach a wing-span of up to just over eleven feet (three meters).

They can keep on gliding on their wings for a year; making a dive now and then into the ocean to catch a fish.

And, then there's such an incredible number of different kinds of other birds, large, small and all the colours.

I could line up many more different kinds of let's call it, examples of what are a minimal part of the myriad of miracles with which God 'populated' our planet, after the Creation, when HE said 'Be' and there was probably like an explosion when everything HE imagined 'Became'.

## 1.19 GOD'S LAW OF 'CAUSE AND EFFECT' AND 'THE BOOK OF DEEDS'

God's Divine Law of 'Cause and Effects' (*'what we sow – we shall reap'* ) is remarkable because through it each human being receives – what he/she deserves - at the exact time, with precise measure. With this Law - God has control of everything every human being does, says and even thinks.

This is all recorded in the respective *'Book of Deeds'* of each individual, to be at the disposition of God on Judgment Day. There's No Escape.

In the Qur'an 17:13-14 God reveals that *'HE made every individual to be fully responsible for his own actions.'*

*On Resurrection Day God will bring forth to each person a book, which will be wide open. It will be said, 'Read your book (of Deeds), because what you find therein, will be enough to identify your own actions, for which you will be held accountable on that Day.'*

# 1.20 GOD APPOINTED A GUARDIAN ANGEL TO EACH SOUL!

In Qur'an 82:10-12 God teaches *that HE has appointed a guardian angel over each one of us, who are noble writers, who record everything we do* (in the respective Book of Deeds – which contains the record of everything we have ever done).

In Qur'an 81:7-14 it is said, 'When the souls will be reunited with their bodies. When the record (each individual 'Book of Deeds') will be opened. When the Hell will be seen ablaze and Paradise will be brought near. Then each soul shall know what it brought.'

In Qur'an 84:7-15 God says. "On the Day of Accountability, he who will be given his Book of Deeds in his right hand shall have an easy time. But he, who is given his Book of Deeds from behind his back in his left hand, would like to be dead. Know that God was ever watching his wrongdoings.'

In Qur'an 86:4, 8-9 it is said that every soul has a guardian angel appointed to him/her.

God's mention of guardian angels who record everything tells us that everything we have ever done, said or thought s being recorded in our respective '*Book of Deeds*'. Nothing's left out.

## 1.21 WHAT GOD TOLD MOSES AT THE BURNING BUSH, ABOUT THE END

When we open our minds to accept the fact that the Qur'an was authored by the Almighty, All-knowing All-seeing, the only living God - for Whom time doesn't exist - gives us an understanding of His immense powers and outreach to see the past and the future.

We get the best example of this, from what HE says in the Qur'an that HE said to Moses at their first encounter, when God attracted Moses to the Burning Bush, some Three-thousand four-hundred years ago.

Qur'an 20:11-15. When Moses reached the bush, a voice said, 'O Moses, I am your God. Listen to what I am about to disclose. I am God, and there is no other God. Therefore, worship only Me.

God went on telling Moses the following that I view to be of special importance to know, which is why I have separated it from the above. God said to Moses, '*The final hour is sure to come. I have decided to keep it hidden* (when the-End-of-Time is going to take place), *so that every soul may be rewarded according to its efforts.*

'*According to its efforts*' means how each individual has gone about its life here on earth to fulfil its purpose (and beyond).

# 1.22 "NO ONE WILL ENTER PARADISE WITHOUT TRIAL", SAID GOD

This is yet another remarkable revelation of God in regards to what HE demands and requires from each one of us to enable us to enter Paradise.

In Qur'an 2:213 God poses the question whether we think that we will enter Paradise without having to stand trial.

Qur'an 2:154. What God says in regards to the above is of fundamental importance. HE declares that HE will test the steadfastness of those individuals who HE (in his judgment) decides are worth it – to be tested in different ways - such as with illness, fear and famine, with loss of property, loss of life and produce.

Those (very few) *who endure the testing with patience, who distressed with their misfortune, say,* 'we belong to God and to Him we shall return' will be in good standing.

God makes it clear that we all will stand in front of Him on Judgment Day, to be judged for what we did while here on earth.

In this revelation HE makes clear that HE is testing us (those of us who HE finds worthy of it) prior to death, to define our steadfastness, relative to our belief in Him, the Only Living God.

Through Isaiah 65:7, God said, "*I will punish them (mankind) as they deserve.*" Not believing in Him and worshipping and obeying His Commandments is a mayor sin.

Those who think they will evade trial at Judgment Day, such as through the invented Christian 'Rapture', not mentioned anywhere in the Jewish Bible or in the Qur'an, are in error; but Satan, our Nemesis, who deceived them to believe it, is happy they think so.

I happen to have read an older Christian Bible wherein nothing was written about how the people would disappear, all of the sudden, as written in newer editions, thus confirming that this is a later day's man-made addition.

# CHAPTER 2

# GOD'S CREATION OF ADAM LED TO THE BECOMING OF SATAN

Satan has done an extraordinary job concealing himself from mankind.
Now it's too late to undo the huge damage
he has caused to mankind throughout the Millennia.
Hopefully a few people will want to listen to what God has said,
which I've worked hard to bring out in the open,
and so, change your ways of thinking and being,
turning to Him, and worshiping only Him, the only living God,
asking (in your Hearts) for guidance and forgiveness.
The invention that God has a son, was masterminded by Satan;
taking away all Christians from the Way of God.

B efore getting started, I want to again underline that it's of the essence that we (every individual) work with determination to change our ways of what and how we think of God.

HE has existed since the '*Beginning of Time*', and is The Uncontested Only Living God. HE is the Almighty Creator and thus the Owner of the Universe. His Powers are far beyond anything you and I can imagine.

It is vitally important to know that Satan exists as well. He has no power, but is a master in what I want to call it, '*the art of deceit*' to deceive mankind, which gives him power over those who listen to him and accept his invitations.

We need to know that God lets us do anything we please to do. Knowing this, Satan dedicates himself incessantly - 24/7 – to deceive us to fall away from the 'narrow way' of God.

Not believing in God and that HE is the Only Living God, causes a sin that takes us away from Him. God has given mankind – let's call it *'information'* - through a multitude of Prophecies or Revelations - to learn from – warning us about our future!

Look around. What do you see? It's a thoroughly corrupted World in crisis, without any possibility of going back, as the result of the effects of the Global Warming that's out of control, getting worse by the minute!

How has it become this way? It is a very long and complex story that began as far back as at God's creation of Adam.

The culprit for it all to happen is our Nemesis and archenemy, Satan – the deceiver – also called *'the prince of this world'*, who lives in the unseen, who is now *'in charge of our world'*.

In the Qur'an God reveals with great detail who Satan is and how he came to be. It was shortly after God's creation of Adam - when Satan – our declared enemy and Nemesis came to be. This is something that's critically important to know. Satan has existed along the Millennia - since long before mankind. What he doesn't know about the human being isn't worth knowing.

The very bad news is that he has been extraordinarily successful in making man to fall in his cleverly disguised traps of deceit, away from the *'narrow way'* of God.

God created Adam (mankind) with a 'free will', which means that man (he/she) is *'free'* to do what he/she wants to do with our lives, of which Satan knows and takes advantage of it.

A *'free will'* might seem as a great gift, but has been and is to the detriment of mankind; because of how we've used it.

Satan has studied mankind, every step we take, how we think and behave. Since he exists in the unseen, where we can't see him, it has given him a tremendous advantage. He is right beside every individual he chooses to be with, because he knows all his shortcomings, which he uses to deceive him or her.

Satan has worked diligently to keep the 'information' about his existence concealed from us. How could he do it? It's easy for him, knowing how man (we) behaves, especially the vainglorious, conceited, arrogant, self-important, narcissistic, inflated, controlling Priesthoods; Satan knows them far better than they – *who (unknowingly) have become his 'puppets' - know themselves,* for the simple reason that they don't understand!

Satan *'influences'* what I call - *'our wants'* – in our minds, causing a majority of us *'to want'* what he wants us *'to want'*; without us having the slightest idea of what's going on.

How is it possible that mankind has so totally disregarded the existence of Satan?

From where did the Roman Catholic Church get the idea that Satan had been an angel, Lucifer, who they say, opposed God?

You can be sure that Satan was right at their side, making certain that they listened to him and adopted the ideas he induced into their minds.

A truly important question I make is, how come there's no mention of importance in the TORAH in the Jewish Bible about Satan, other than that he deceived Adam and Eve – causing them to disobey God? Why did God not – as it looks - provide revelations of Satan in the TORAH, similar to what HE provides in the Qur'an?

From the foregoing in Chapter 1, we have learned that God is angry with most of mankind. HE has foretold that HE will punish our planet *'and us'* with terrible punishments, the last of which will be *'Supernatural in nature'* that can't be explained.

In the Book of Revelation 15:1 John written that he saw seven angels with seven plagues, which were *'the Final Manifestation'* for the anger of God.

According to God's revelations in mainly the Books of Revelation and in Daniel, our last years will be so disastrous that it goes beyond our imagination to picture what will happen.

Satan has been the driver of the demise of mankind, with the acceptance of God. Since mostly nobody believes in the existence of Satan – that he is real - it's really irrelevant what anybody believes. But, this is what God has revealed in the Qur'an!

As we are learning, everything we need to know about Satan is taught by God in great detail in the Qur'an.

God discloses that the angels HE created of '*pure white light*', and that '*HE didn't grant them a free will*'. I'm convinced that God made this disclosure about His Angels, in order that those who invented the notion that angels went against God, know that they can't oppose their Creator. Thus, there goes the story of the Roman Catholic Church up in smoke.

In order to get an understanding of God and His Creation of man, it's '*a must*' to read the Qur'an. Don't question if it's 'good or bad' – just read it. Being that it was authored by God, it can only be good. It's the Book that will help anybody who honestly wants to find God – to find Him.

I've learned that Christian Priesthoods teach Christians that the Qur'an is '*of demonic origin*' and therefore evil. This is a terrible lie. Satan is of course very happy for this.

The Qur'an is the Book of God – a remarkable Book - that contains information that the Christian 'Leaderships' don't want their Christians followers to learn about.

Every time I open the Qur'an, I become marvelled about the remarkable words and passages that God wrote; for the guidance of mankind. The Qur'an – as mentioned - is the only place that provides the detailed story of the creation of Adam provided by God – that's of fundamental importance to learn about.

As mentioned in my sub-chapter 1.14, the reason the Qur'an came to be - was because of what God revealed through the Prophet Jeremiah 8:7-9 (narrated above in detail) that His LAW (the TORAH – God's first Book of the LAW) *have been changed*. It's obvious that God couldn't and can't accept that '*His Words*' were changed - largely eradicated.

It's doubtless one of the absolutely most important revelations that God made when HE over and over narrates the detailed story about His creation of Adam – and how Satan - the evil terrible Nemesis of man - came to be. It wasn't because he rebelled against God in a way that could be called 'a Power-play' as the Roman Catholic Church teaches.

I say that if God had wanted - HE could have killed Satan on the spot, simply by thinking him dead. Which Satan knows.

As I believe, God gave Satan respite to be around until '*The Day of Resurrection*', which he asked for, as God revealed in Qur'an 15:36, and is using Satan to test the faith of mankind towards Him.

Because we can't see him, mankind hasn't been able to grasp that the unseen Satan is real. He is an extremely clever being who deceived the early Jewish Priesthood to eliminate mentions of him – who he is and what he told to God that he would do to mankind – at the time most probably when the TORAH went into Print.

It's his hatred against mankind, the offspring of Adam that's affecting man - and our planet – that's on a steady course to soon cease to be a unique living planet.

The ancient Revelations in the Jewish Bible and in the Qur'an were intended as Guidance and Warnings, to alert mankind of a coming Terrible Ending – that's on course to take mankind to '*The Day of Resurrection*' and *Judgment Day*.

At that time - that's rapidly approaching – God, as HE has revealed, will bring back to life the bodies of all people who died through the ages to reunite them with the respective souls.

This will happen when we stand trial for what we did with our lives while on earth. I will refer to texts from Genesis 1 and 2

in the Jewish Bible and from the Qur'an chapters 2, 7, 15, 20 and 38 that that complement one another.

Texts comparable to those in the Qur'an related to the Creation of Adam – how it happened - do not exist in the Jewish TORAH. I believe however that God gave the texts to Moses to become part of the TORAH. I'm convinced – as mentioned before - that it wasn't '*dishonest scribes*' who were responsible for the eradications, but some '*dishonest*' High-ranking Jewish Rabbi(s), who ordered Scribes to do it.

## 2.1 THE CREATION OF ADAM – AS WRITTEN IN THE JEWISH BIBLE

Reference is made to the Book of Genesis in the Jewish Bible when God told His angels that HE was going to create human beings that would look like Him. And so, God formed a man out of the soil (dust) of the ground and breathed life-giving breath into his nostrils giving Adam life. That's the extent of what's said in the Jewish Bible about the creation of Adam.

When God speaks of Himself, HE does it often in His Majestic plural tense, as 'We', 'Us' and 'Our'. This has been misconceived by some to think that HE was speaking of Himself and of somebody else, which isn't true.

But it gave some (the Roman Catholic Priesthood, after it came to be in the year 325 AD) the idea that God was talking of Jesus, and thus that he existed since the beginning of time, as the son of God.

As we shall learn, this is incorrect, because God, the Majesty of the Universe, was talking of Himself. Texts from the Qur'an complement and amplify the above ones from the TORAH.

## 2.2 GOD'S CREATION OF ADAM – LED TO THE BECOMMING OF SATAN

Revelations from the following chapters: Qur'an 2:[30–39], 7:[11–18], 7:[189-198], 14:[22], 15:[26-44], *20:[116-120], 38:[71-88]* are of the essence to know and learn to understand.

The Qur'an contains both guidance and outright warnings directed to mankind. Very important to know is that God repeatedly warns about Satan, how he would deceive mankind making it (us) to go to perdition! Very unfortunately for all of us, Satan - the deceiver - has been so astute that he managed to convince mankind to negate his existence. In the story of His creation of Adam, provided below, God offers detailed information and warnings about Satan.

When I learned about what God says of how Satan came to be, I realized that this is something that every human being should know it. I have said it before and want to say again that it's remarkable that nothing is ever said about Satan. It is as if religious people, priests and other are afraid of saying anything about him. Silence, silence about him, while Satan is having a great time deviating the great majority of mankind away from God.

As we shall learn in the following, Satan is a being who lives in the unseen on another dimension. He sees the human beings and knows everything that's going on with each one of us. He could be right beside you listening to you and is able to induce thoughts into your mind in such a way that it seems to be something you thought yourself - which is to your liking - but certainly not to God.

What God says in the Qur'an is awesome and should be known by every human being to enable us to withstand the manipulations of Satan.

I would have liked to transfer (copy) the many revelations that God provided in the Qur'an into this Sub-Chapter, but that would get me into 'Copyright' issues with the people who made the respective translations of the original Arabic Qur'an. In any case however, it seems to me, since I have a good handle of the English Language (as well as of Spanish and Swedish) and know the Jewish Bible in-depth that a good many of the translations don't do a good job in replicating what it was that God said, as I believe my Story will.

God announced to His angels that HE was going to create a man from black mud - moulded in His image - and breath into him of His Spirit.

God talked through His Prophet Mohammad, to whom HE said that HE told His angels HE was going to *place* a deputy *on earth HE also told him* that before Adam, HE created another species in His image from smokeless fire, who HE named Jinn.

We learn that the Arabic word Jinn derives from the verb "*Janna*, which means '*to hide*'. In Islamic literature, Shaitân (Satan) was the name given to disbelieving Jinns who don't obey or believe in God.

We can't see the Jinn, because they live in the unseen, on another dimension, although they see us and can be right beside us.

We learn that both man and Jinn were given a '*free will*', allowing us and them to do as they please with their lives.

*As God has revealed in the Qur'an, HE created His angels of pure white light and* didn't bestow them a '*free will*'. Therefore, it is impossible for an angel to turn against God; or to disobey Him in any way, as the story of the Roman Catholic Church tells it.

We learn that God taught Adam the names of all angels. HE presented Adam to the angels and Jinn and told Adam to *tell them their names*. After that Adam had told the angels their names, God told (ordered) the angels and Jinn, *to bow down to Adam* (to show their respect for his great knowledge). All bowed down, except a Jinn, by the name Iblis who refused to bow to Adam.

I say, how many of us don't commit errors - over and over - in our arrogance that takes us away from God.

God asked Iblis what prevented him from prostrating himself to one who HE had created with His Hands? Was he too proud to prostrate to Adam or did he think he could do as he pleased?

Iblis responded that he was better than Adam, for the reason that God had created him from smoke-free fire, while God created Adam from dirt. We observe that Iblis looked down on God's creation of the man who was made from dirt.

God ordered Iblis - the new become Satan - to get out from His presence, making him an outcast. God told Iblis that His curse was on him till the Day of Resurrection (the Day when mankind and Jinn will be brought to God for Final Judgment).

We learn that Iblis (Satan) despite, of what had happened, kept being respectful to God, when he asked to be given 'respite till the Day of Resurrection.'

It's evident that since Iblis/Satan - directed himself to God with respect, there's no doubt that he knew '*his place*'!

God 'granted Satan a stay before his punishment went into effect'), until the Day of Resurrection.

It is important to understand that Iblis, the new become Satan was condemned but was allowed by God to continue '*to be around*' until the Day of Resurrection.

This has been (is) to the detriment of mankind.

The following statements made by Satan to God - and God's response to him – in accordance to the Qur'an, are of paramount importance that every human being needs to know.

Satan answered to God (being most respectful) that since he had been given respite, he was going to mislead all human beings except '*His chosen slaves*' (those who believe in God).

Satan declared to God that he would lay in wait on the human beings. He would ensnare them and make them *fall away from 'The Straight Way' of God, coming* upon them from in-front and from behind, from their right and their left. Satan told God that HE would find out that most of them would be unthankful to Him and that not many would be left on His '*Straight Way*'.

This is a vitally important matter to know and understand. The new-become Satan became man's instant enemy (it was because of man that God cursed Iblis/Satan). Satan wowed to God that he was going to go after the human beings – the slaves of God - and destroy all those who weren't God's *chosen slaves*.

God told Satan that he would have no authority over His slaves (mankind), except those who followed him (Satan) (non-believers, polytheists [those who believe in and worship several gods], criminals and evil-doers). Hell was the place that was guaranteed for all of them.

God declared to Satan that HE *would fill Hell with him* (Satan) *and all those who followed him.*

This is yet another critically important revelation of God, wherein God told Satan that HE (God) allowed Satan to go after the human beings as he pleased (free from restraints).

Satan answered God that HE *would find most of them (the human beings) to be unthankful (ungrateful).* In other words, we (human beings) are ungrateful to God because we don't realize that we have Him to thank for the life HE gave us. We don't take Him into account and worship only Him – the only Living God - thanking only Him - as HE deserves - for the life HE gave to each and one of us.

God told Adam that he and his wife were to live in Paradise, and eat of everything as they wished. But HE warned them not to approach a certain tree. If they did, and eat of it, both of them would become sinners (for disobeying Him).

We learn that Satan has no power of his own over human beings. God reveals that he (Satan) - only invites – and people who like his ideas (with no thought about the next life) accept them - thereby falling away from God's "*Right Way*".

God, the All-knowing, revealed what Satan will say on Judgment Day, when we (mankind and Jinn) stand in front of Him to be judged for what we did while here on earth. I suggest that you look up on the Internet what Satan will say, as revealed by God.

My observation is that in this revelation (and so many other) that God made in the Qur'an - when HE tells what Satan will say, close to fourteen hundred and some years later. It's the same, as with so many of God's revelations about our future that are 'Proof' of His memory and mind-blowing Powers, how HE could see into what we call a distant future, which was thousands of years away.

Not only could (can) God see our future – HE knows exactly what is going to happen and be (going to be) said at that time (and at any time) – by anybody.

I want to emphasize this matter, so we have a better understanding of Him, the Only Living God!

Note that in the exchange of words between God and Satan, God referred to us (as did Satan) as 'the children of Adam' (mankind) as '*His slaves*' and not as 'His children'.

In the Qur'an God says so many things of importance for mankind - relative to everything – some of which is mentioned in the Jewish Bible (Old Testament). What HE states in the following is of fundamental importance for each one of us to know.

God makes a question wherein HE asks if we think that HE created us without giving us a purpose and if we would never return to Him for Accountability.

It's clear, isn't it? We – every one of us - were given a purpose, but it's up to each one of us to find and work on it.

We shall return to the Almighty God on *the Day of Judgment* - when we all will resurrect with human bodies - as programmed by God – to return to Him.

Having a human body when in Hell is very different from being only a soul, because the pain and suffering felt by the human body will be excruciatingly terrible.

At that time – on Judgment Day - you, and me, and everybody, and as we just learned - also Satan - will be held accountable before God for our actions – for all that we did, said and even thought - while living on Earth.

As mentioned, God says in the Qur'an that every believer will have its steadfastness tested to make sure that he (she) deserves entering His Kingdom. And, we will be asked to render accounts for what we did to fulfil the purpose HE designated to each of us.

The rich, will be held accountable in regards to how you used your wealth, why you didn't use - at least some of it - to help the less fortunate, the poor, the sick (for instance by donating to the St. Jude's

Children's Hospital), donate to children with special needs. Think about the elderly (Donate to AARP to help the elderly to have a better life) donate to help people who lost everything in Natural Disasters (as we see so many increasingly occurring all around the planet). Become involved, show interest, become part of the help-activities that will result from your donations.

What will you answer to God – The Great Judge – when it is your turn to stand in-front of Him on Judgment Day when HE asks; '*what did you do with the life I gave you?*'

Everything that took place in our lives here on earth becomes written in our personal 'Book of Deeds' by our respective guardian angel. There's no possibility to hide or negate anything we did.

When you stand in front of Him, HE will instantly know everything that's written in your Book.

Nothing will escape Him about you, about me, about every one of us, and consequently, '*as we did sow so will we be rewarded*'.

## 2.3 IT'S OF THE ESSENCE TO KNOW THAT SATAN EXISTS

I cannot repeat this enough. Learning about Satan, who he is, and that he exists, is of paramount importance for mankind. Because, in the same way, that many people don't believe in the Existence of God, most people don't think that Satan is real.

Satan does exist and works untiringly 24/7 to 'kick' as many of us as he can, *from 'The Straight Way' of God*, before Judgment Day – that's closing in on us, very fast! Satan has an army of 'devils' at his disposition, working with him to corrupt us.

Mankind has become lost in a world (our planet) that we think we dominate, while the truth is, we don't. Instead, we have become *'puppets'* of Satan, the ones that he dominates in every way imaginable and unimaginable.

You won't probably believe what I will say, and it is that it's evident that God has taken away His hands from us. This is so because mankind disregards Him - by living sinful immoral lives – such as that of gay and lesbian individuals who have been accepted by governments to gain their votes, as well as by many churches.

But in the Book of Leviticus in the Jewish Bible, it's said that men are not *to have sexual relations with one another because God hates it.* This is also valid for women. It's also said that men who have *sexual relations shall be put to death.* There's absolutely no way to misunderstand what's said herein!

In the Book of Romans in The New Testament it's written that women, who pervert the natural use of their sex by unnatural acts, will be punished.

Be aware that politicians (governments) who legalize what's unacceptable to God; make themselves sinners, to be severely punished as well.

In various chapters in the Book of Revelation sexual immorality is defined several times as unacceptable.

You can be sure that Satan made this to happen by inducing corrupting ideas into the minds of the lawmakers who made same-sex marriage lawful (to get their votes). It is therefore vital to understand who Satan is and why he hates us. And, how come man has become '*a puppet*' of Satan, who pulls our '*strings*' as he wills.

In a quote of famous French writer Baudelaire, he asserted that "*The Devil's cleverest wile has been to convince mankind – that he doesn't exist, while he watches us from the unseen with his baleful eyes.*" And he has been exceedingly successful!

I've thought that if Satan could die, the only way it could happen would be by chocking from all his laughing of how easy it has been and is, to make man to fall in his traps of deceit.

Satan often called '*the prince of our world*' (Planet Earth) is in charge with explicit permission (as we have learned) from God to do as he pleases with mankind. But, as God told Satan, *everybody who follows him, will go with him to Hell.*

God wants man to decide by our own '*free will*' to walk 'on *His Narrow Way of Righteousness*', obeying His Commandments.

Today, the popular way on which most humans like to walk is '*the broad way*' – '*the way of Satan*' – that's taking the corrupted souls to Hell.

It's of the essence that we understand that - as I believe - God doesn't involve Himself in the individual 'affairs' of man – as many people seem to believe, when they say things like "*Oh G--, why have you done this, so and so to me.*"

God requires man to turn to Him and only Him and worship Him 'Always' – '*several times Every Day*' not just when things go bad. HE is – according to His First Commandment – the Only God to be worshiped, Who can help!

Trough the Prophet Isaiah, God teaches that besides Him, there's no other god, there never was and never will be. Thus, no other living god has ever existed!

Understand that when you accept an 'invitation' from Satan, it causes you to fall away from "*the Way*" of the Only Living God – our Creator.

What does the Creation of Adam have anything to do with "The End of Our Time"?

It's the appearance of Satan on the scenario at the Creation of Adam that introduced the '*element of evil*' to which man so easily falls and perverts himself. Man 'is free' to choose what he wants and – unfortunately - most of the time he (man) chooses the broad evil wrong ways into which Satan so easily ensnares man.

I want to again remind you of God's Divine Karmic LAW of "*Cause and Effect*". Everything we do, say and even think causes an effect we can't escape. "*What we sow – we shall reap.*"

Most importantly, we need to also understand that what a human being causes, affects "Mother Earth" individually and collectively. How is it possible, you ask?

The fact that God created man using the soil of the Earth (to which it will return) is of immeasurable consequence to our planet.

It is, as I see it, the key to understanding why - as the world population grows - what we all do = our actions = affects our planet, "*Mother Earth*", in more and more powerful ways.

Being that '*man was made of the soil of the earth*', in point of fact means that our bodies are an integral part of "*Mother Earth*". Interesting, isn't it!

An exponentially growing population which has reached about eight Billion inhabitants - has become a significant part of Mother Earth. The compounded actions of mankind transcend as evil Karmic (negative) energy that affects the unseen spiritual level.

All of this is known by Satan, our Nemesis, as he indefatigably works to make man fall in his seductive traps!

From the above we've learned how enormously astute, cunning and ingenious Satan, man's unseen Enemy is – as he causes – mankind – '*his puppets*'- to fall in his carefully arranged '*traps of perdition*'. He is far more ingenious than anybody can comprehend.

We need to be aware that Satan has had thousands of years to '*sharpen his weapons of deceit*' against man, his enemy by his choice, because of his hatred against us. And he knows – to perfection – how to lead us towards perdition.

In the Qur'an, we find that God time after time admonishes the offspring of Adam and warns '*the children of Adam*', about Satan and of the consequences of following the ideas he induces into us.

God, who sees Satan (while Satan can't see God) and knows that he is out to take down mankind, never admonishes him. Why is that? We need to return to the moment after the creation of Adam when God gave respite to Satan until the End.

From the unseen, where Satan lives, he (and his army of devils) has the ability to interfere '*our feeble minds*' with '*seductive corrupting ideas*' that are induced into us without that we have the slightest idea of what has been done to us.

The best way for Satan to deceive man away from *God's Narrow Path* is, to make man invent religions that worship anybody or anything that isn't the Only Living God.

Satan has succeeded in extraordinary ways because all religions, except the two that were originated by God, depart from the stringent requirements of His LAWS and Commandments.

We shall return to this. But even the only two religions, which God originated - Judaism and Islam - have received serious 'dents', resulting from the activities of deceit of Satan.

You ask, what about the Christian Trinity religion? I say No HE didn't!

Jesus taught strict adherence to the teachings and the LAW of God wherein HE requires total adherence to His Commandments to worship Him alone, the Only Living God. In the Qur'an HE says, "Don't say trinity," which very clearly shows his stance!

But God's Commandments and teachings were not adhered to because the original religion, as taught by Jesus – and all previous Prophets of God - was changed to follow a man-made Trinity religion with three god-heads. The modified 'man-made' Christianity put in place in the Year 325 was defined by what is known as the Nicene Creed at the Bishops Ecumenical Conference at Nicaea in Turkey.

Satan - the deceiver – took the opportunity whispering in the minds of the Christian Priesthood of the new Roman Catholic Church, the need to create a Christian Bible. It was to include the Jewish Bible naming it '*The Old Testament*'. By virtue of its name, it became relegated to a less important place, becoming more something of unimportant historical significance, rather than religious.

The important part, from the viewpoint of the new Christian Trinity religion became named '*The New Testament*' that defined the religious teachings of the Catholic Church; the Jewish Bible no more to be valid. What an enormous triumph for Satan!

# 2.4 GOD FORMED EVE FROM A RIB OF ADAM REVELATIONS FROM THE JEWISH BIBLE AND THE QUR'AN.

Eve, the woman, man's companion, God created in the Garden of Eden. God made Adam fall into a deep sleep. While he was sleeping, God took out one of the man's ribs and closed up the flesh. We learn that God formed the woman out of the rib and brought her to Adam. He was happy to see one of his kind and called her 'woman', because she was taken out of man. They were both naked, but weren't embarrassed.

God told Adam to dwell with his wife in Paradise. They could eat any fruit they pleased, but never eat the fruit of a certain tree. If they did – God warned - both would become wrongdoers.

We learn that God addressed Adam and warned him about Satan that he who was an enemy to Adam and his wife. God told Adam not to let Satan get him and his wife out of Paradise, which would cause suffering. In Paradise, the two of them were not going to be hungry. Nor were they to suffer from thirst or from heat.

As we observe, God addressed Adam. Eve was surely also there, listening to God, when HE said that they were not *to approach the tree and eat of it because both would become wrongdoers"*.

It is astounding that God warned them about Satan, as we learn -because he was their enemy - and that despite thereof they fell for his seductive talk.

The consequence, as we know, was that mankind - their offspring lost Paradise, as punishment for their sin, disobeying their creator.

## 2.5 "CHILDREN OF ADAM" BE AWARE OF SATAN – YOUR REAL ENEMY

God created Adam as His slave, to become His servant, as also we, his offspring. Nowhere does God call Adam or any of his offspring – '*My children*'. Instead, in the Qur'an God calls them '*children of Adam*'.

God said. *Children of Adam! We gave you clothing to cover yourselves* (your private parts) *and as an adornment.*

HE told the *Children of Adam to be careful and avoid that* Satan, their open enemy, *deceived them, as he* did with their *parents* [Adam and Eve], which caused them to be expelled from paradise; *when Satan - them unknowing - stripped their parents of their clothing.*

# 2.6 ADAM AND EVE FELL FOR THE DECEITFUL LIES OF SATAN

From the Qur'an we learn that Shaitãn (Satan) approached Adam, whispering to him that he would take *him to the Tree of Immortality. He told Adam that the reason Almighty God forbid him to approach the tree was because HE wanted to prevent him and Eve from becoming angels or immortals.*

Satan swore to them that he was their *sincere adviser*, and they believed him, thus showing how shrewd he was in seducing them.

After they ate from the tree, they became aware of their nakedness and began to cover themselves with leaves from the garden. Thus did Adam and Eve disobey the Almighty God and became sinners.

Observe that God provided the information in the Qur'an of what really had happened, because HE knew that what's written in Genesis about this matter is incorrect.

From this revelation - made by God - we observe that Satan addressed Adam (not Eve, as the story goes in the Book of Genesis in the Bible), but then the text goes on to say, "*He swore to them both and they believed him.*" As we see, there are important discrepancies here. We find that Satan directed himself to Adam, not to Eve, although she was there as well.

In the Book of Genesis, it's written that as soon as they had eaten the fruit, they were given 'understanding', whereupon they realized that they were naked; so, they sewed fig leaves together and covered themselves.

God called out to them. Without seeing them, His extraordinary senses told Him what had happened.

God told them HE had forbid them to approach the tree and that HE had warned them about Satan, who was their 'open enemy'.

This is basically what is written in the Book of Genesis.

The difference, however, is that in Genesis in the Jewish Bible Satan is described to be a snake, which he wasn't in accordance to what God reveals in the Qur'an!

In Genesis its written that God cursed Satan, and told him that from that moment on, he would have to crawl on his belly and eat dust as long as he lived.

Even if it doesn't matter at this time, we observe that what's written in the Book of Genesis in the Jewish Bible, deviates strongly from what God has revealed in the Qur'an; what really occurred with Satan. And, we know that God is HE Who knows the best.

I'm convinced that Satan messed it up for the Jewish priesthood, when they were putting together the Book of Genesis in their Bible, which created many discrepancies to what God has revealed in the Qur'an.

## 2.7 ADAM AND EVE ASKED GOD TO FORGIVE THEM THEIR SIN

A Critically Important Revelation of God.

From the Qur'an we learn that Adam and Eve repented and that Adam asked God that HE have mercy on them and forgive them their great sin. If HE didn't, they would be losers.

We learn, which is important to know, God chose to accept their repentance and gave them guidance. But HE told them to get out from Paradise, all of them, Adam, Eve and also Satan – Iblis the former Jinn, which I believe happened in a matter of an instant.

God said that they would remain enemies to one another.

He also told them that whenever there came guidance from Him, whosoever followed His guidance, would *never get into trouble.*

But HE alerted them that the one who turned away from Him, would live a miserable life, and be raised back to life by Him as a blind person on the Day of Resurrection."

It's a vital revelation of what man is to expect in his life in the *'Hereafter'*, which depends on how we relate to God, the Only Living God, the Creator of all, while in this life.

This was the first indication of how cunning Satan was (is) - when he tempted Adam and Eve in Paradise - *'basically in the presence of God'* - making them fall even though God had warned them about Satan. Thus, Satan immediately began to fulfil his promise to God – that he would make mankind to fall away from *'His Straight Way'*!

My reflection is that Adam and Eve were lucky to be forgiven on the spot by their Creator, for their sin. But, very tragically for mankind, we have had to pay a huge price for their disobedience to God, resulting from Satan when he led them astray – such as he has done with most of mankind ever since.

Satan already once managed to corrupt mankind so much that God annihilated it through 'the Deluge'. If we think about it, it's impressive. Only Noah and his family were left.

Satan was without a job for some time. We can be sure that he went after the new human beings - the offspring of Noah - with a vengeance; and we can see the results in the rapidly growing destructive effects of the Global warming.

This time around with Judgment Day getting close, those who have disobeyed God will not be as lucky as Adam and Eve. Because, *there's no forgiveness to expect once entering that Day!*

## 2.8 GOD FORGAVE ADAM AND EVE THEIR SIN, BUT EVICTED THEM FROM PARADISE AS PUNISHMENT AND SIMULTANEOUSLY ALSO SATAN

### There was NO remaining Sin that required an 'offer-lamb'!

God's revelation in the Qur'an of His forgiveness of Adam and Eve is of fundamental importance. This is because it means that (as mentioned before) there was no remaining '*Original Sin of man (Adam)*' that would require mankind to be 'cleansed' by use of an 'Offer Lamb'.

The '*Original Sin*' is a notion that was invented by the Roman Catholic Church, as so many other like the one quoted below from the Book of Revelation.

As we learn from this revelation, Adam and Eve were forgiven. Yes, they were forgiven, according to God Himself. Therefore, the idea that an 'offer-lamb' was needed to obtain forgiveness for a '*sin that God had forgiven*' was clearly a man-made one.

God punished Adam and Eve for having disobeyed him. Evicting them from Paradise, where they had enjoyed an 'easy-going' life, to the harsh reality of life outside was a terrible change.

The importance of this unique revelation is that since there was No remaining sin left to cleanse, there was no need for an 'Offer Lamb' – Jesus – who, in accordance with God, HE didn't allow that to happen.

The All-knowing God knows this since HE reveals in the Qur'an that Jesus wasn't killed. So, then the question is how come that in the New Testament and the Book of Revelation Jesus repeatedly is named to be the Lamb?

God having revealed that HE forgave Adam and Eve for their sin against Him – from His perspective, as I see it – '*the case of Adam's and Eve's sin against Him was closed*'. There was no need for an 'offer-lamb' as invented by the Roman Catholics.

God's revelations in the Qur'an about Satan – that he wasn't an angel – and that HE evicted him from Paradise simultaneously with Adam and Eve - are of fundamental importance.

It is so, because it provides evidence that what's written in the Book of Revelation 12:7-8 that says that war broke out in heaven when the archangel Michael fought against the dragon and his angels.

My question is - where did this story come from? I state that it's impossible that John wrote it!

Whoever was holding the pen to write it, doubtless had good help from Satan - the deceiver - who must have been '*out of himself*' to be able to so thoroughly confuse the minds of the priesthood of the new Roman Catholic Church, when it took on to write their Christian New Testament based on a trinity godhead.

I can see Satan, just about '*laughing himself to death*'.

Since Satan can't see the future – as only does God – I'm convinced that he had no idea of the colossal damage he caused to mankind. Now he knows and is more than happy that so many human beings will soon be making him company in Hell.

## 2.9 WHO ARE WE (MAN) IN REALITY?

The matter of '*who we are*' is of fundamental importance to know, to get the right perspective relative to our origin and how that affects our planet and our Destiny.

God has no spouse – therefore - HE has no children. As we learned above, Adam was created by God from the soil of the earth, therefore we aren't children of God - we are the offspring of Adam and Eve, as HE repeatedly clarifies in the Qur'an – but we are also - children of "Mother Earth".

Christians have been taught and teach that man is a child of God. But in essential parts of the Jewish Bible and in the Qur'an, we are told that God created man - to be His slaves.

From the Book of Revelation, we learn that John fell down on his knees to worship an angel who had talked with him. John says that the angel told him not to do that because he was a slave (of God), as was John. Only God was to be worshipped, the angel told John.

This is a crucial statement on the part of the angel because that is what we are - humans and angels - slaves and (intended) servants of God, Who created man and to Whom we all belong – and to Whom we all shall return on 'Judgment Day' also called *'Dooms Day', 'The Day of Accountability'*, and also *'The Day of Regret'*.

Said this, we must urgently begin to teach the Truth to enable at least some people to get out of the snares of Satan, to *the Narrow Way of Righteousness* of the Only Living God, the Almighty Creator, Ruler, Master and Owner of All.

Among many things, God declares in the Qur'an – that *'HE is the Merciful'* – *'the Compassionate'* - *'the Forgiving'*! HE will listen to those who turn to Him and ask in our hearts for forgiveness – as did Adam – and to be guided by Him!

Human beings need to learn the truth and turn exclusively to Him, the Only Living God, in worship and prayer, asking Him and Him alone (no intercessors – because HE doesn't accept any) for guidance, doing what HE 'Commanded' us to do.

In the Qur'an 2:153 God tells us that those who believe in Him alone, to seek His help patiently with prayer, because HE is with those who are patient.

As mentioned before, the fact, as revealed both in the Bible and the Qur'an - that man was created *of the dust of the earth,'* is a crucial revelation. It's vital to understand it because it tells us that man is intimately and directly related to 'Mother Earth'. Materially speaking - we are part of her.

We are 'her children' because we were 'created' of her (not children of God because as HE has revealed throughout the Qur'an HE doesn't have any).

In the Book of Genesis 3:19, it is written that we were taken from the earth because we are dirt and that we shall return to become dirt (as part of "Mother Earth".

It is very clear.

## 2.10 WE HAVE BECOME THE UNKNOWING PUPETS OF A RELENTLESS SATAN

### How could it become this way?

After having gone into the depth of both the Jewish Bible and the Qur'an, I've come to the conclusion that Satan is a being of whom mankind knows nothing. But, at the same time - as ironical as it sounds - he happens to be the one (obviously after God) about whom mankind ought to have tried to learn the most.

The culprits for this were the religious leaders of mainly Christianity and the Jews, who never took initiatives to investigate Satan. They knew of the existence of Satan, but didn't give that knowledge importance.

There exist so many institutions that investigate anything and everything, but not about Satan, if he really exists, or...

I believe Satan is (next to God of course) the cleverest and cunning being in the Universe, who dedicated himself 24/7 to the downfall of mankind.

God is pure goodness; while Satan is the evil himself. It is remarkable that so much time passed since God created Adam and Eve, who shortly after were deceived by Satan into disobeying God and lost their place in Paradise.

Because mankind has been unable to understand that Satan is a real being - as we've learned - he has been able to continue his work of deceit – completely undisturbed. Now that we are just about to reach the end - it doesn't matter what anybody thinks.

Despite of this I'm going to try to bring in some additional words of wisdom related to Satan about how he realizes his evil work, which he has been able to 'fine-tune' to perfection over the millennia.

We are his '*puppets*', whom he treats at his entire will. He doesn't really have to do anything more than to stay attentive to 'catch' as many of us in his '*seemingly nice traps of deceit*'; that he has disguised to perfection.

I see Satan stretched out on a beach in His realm on another dimension, sunbathing having his preferred '*Perfect-for-hell*' drink; his devils meanwhile tele-transport themselves around '*telepathically*' sending him their observations of who is available to be *'the-next-to-fall'* candidate. There is a myriad of devils, who are having *'a-hell-of-a-time'* helping Satan to make us fall.

Satan, instantly tele-transports himself to the site and whispers his enticing ideas to be rich, of the 'nice things' that can be done to win a presidency, to take over the ownership of whatever, to get an undesired competitor out of the way, in whatever way. It will be so easy to take over the beautiful wife of your neighbour. She's bored it'll be easy to make her your lover. That secretary of yours, she's available to be taken out for dinner and for you know what afterwards. How about getting your wife or parents out of the way and inherit a good chunk of money; nobody will know if you do it this way.

And, in regards to the 'ego-riders'; it's important to get a nicer looking house than your neighbours/best friend. How are you going to let him look better than you? Oh, and your car, of course you need to drive a classy looking 'attention-grabbing' one. Is it too expensive? Don't worry, you can handle it.

Oh, there are infinitely many things that can be done to benefit you and have a good time the rest of your life. Don't have second thoughts. Just do it and you'll see!

Satan is a master in inducing his ideas into the minds of people as if they were our own thoughts. The little voice of our consciousness that talked to us when we were kids has become so overpowered by the boastful one of Satan that it's no longer heard.

As I said before, Satan is a master in 'influencing' what I call - *'our wants'* – in our minds, causing us *'to want'* what he wants us *'to want'*; without us having the slightest idea of what's going on.

We never question where any idea came from, or if it's good or bad, or if it's going to have any bad repercussion.

I never heard a priest or preacher mention any such thing; obviously because they are under the dominion of Satan.

Satan's *'ideas of deceit'* are infinite; and amazingly, he always knows precisely what to offer to whom and when.

Because Satan has managed to make so many to be *'his puppets'* - as mentioned before - practically nothing fails for Satan.

He knows to perfection, what 'fits' those of us who he knows are available to his deceitful offers; that range the whole spectrum of evil.

Satan knows that his time to be punished, is closing in very fast, so you can believe that he is putting in a lot of extra effort to make as many of us as possible to fall.

From what can be observed relative to what's happening around the World, Satan is being extremely successful!

# CHAPTER 3
## GOD'S PAST PUNISHMENTS WERE LESSONS TO BE REMEMBERED

W hy is it important to bring up the ancient Biblical episodes of long past events? It is because we need to have in mind that God punished mankind at different occasions for its sinful ways of living. HE demonstrated how with His Immeasurable Powers – impossible for us humans to fathom - HE punished our ancestors in different ways, something that in accordance to His ancient Prophecies is about to happen again – a last time.

As I understand it, HE wanted those occurrences to be narrated and remembered to serve as warnings of what could (is about to) happen to mankind in the future if we didn't change.

Very sadly we never changed due to man's propensity to do what is widely viewed as doing things that are fun, without an idea of the potential consequences.

People in today's World have lost track of how we should live and behave. With atheism and homosexuality, which God despises (as indicated in the foregoing Chapter), but accepted by mankind, and moral values down the drain, a global disaster is in the making.

This chapter is dedicated to the occasions when God punished people for their immoral and evil wicked ways of living.

This time around, God is making mankind to extensively punish itself, as the result of our own sins hitting back on us - like a Boomerang hitting back – caused by what we set in motion – through the effects of the Global Warming.

But at the very end, during the last seven years of our existence - just about to begin - the LORD God foretold as we learn in the Book of Revelation and in the Book of Daniel - that HE will punish mankind with excruciating 'Super-natural' punishments through which it (we) will **be annihilated**.

The plagues with which God punished the Egyptians that are described in the TORAH, in the Book of Exodus Chapters 7 – 12, are similar to those that God has announced that HE will use; as described in the Book of Revelation, Chapters 8 to 16, only that this time around – at our end – the plagues will hit mankind on a global scale.

The occurrences narrated below are taken from the Jewish Bible that God gave '*as critically important reminders*' of how HE punished mankind in ancient times - with horrible deaths.

God punished mankind for its wicked immoral ways of living. Those weren't just stories, but real occurrences that were recorded, for future generations, such as ours; from which we could have learned from, if we had paid attention.

In the Qur'an God provides additional information relative to numerous occurrences narrated in the Jewish Bible that are important to know.

The Final Punishment of mankind is in the process to begin at any moment. It will have similarities to the Egyptian one – but will have a global reach and correspondingly greater power – with far more excruciating agonizing effects that'll be unbearable, as God reveals.

# 3.1 THE DELUGE - BIBLE/GENESIS - GOD 'WIPED OUT' MANKIND

### as the result of its sinful and immoral ways of living.
### (From the Book of Genesis in the Jewish Bible)

Mankind had spread all over the world, and people lived up to the age of close to one thousand years. Then God said (because of their wicked behaviour) that HE would not allow people to live that long because they were mortal. From that moment on they wouldn't live longer than a-hundred-and-twenty years.

The story goes on to say that when God saw how wicked everyone on earth was and how evil their thoughts were at all time, HE decided to wipe out the people HE had created.

But HE was pleased with Noah who had no faults and was the only good man of his time. We learn that God looked at the world and saw that it was evil, because all people were living evil lives.

God told Noah that HE was going to put an end to mankind that HE was going wipe out because of their wickedness. Thereupon, God instructs Noah on how to build the Ark, which took forty years.

Noah was six hundred years old when the flood came on the earth. The sky opened, and rain fell on the earth for forty days and nights. The water became so deep it covered the highest mountains. Al living species on earth died."

When Noah and his ark finally found land, they debarked. God told Noah and his sons to have *many children so that their descendants would live all over the earth. All the animals were placed under their power.*

From this revelation we learn that God intended mankind (His slaves and servants - not His children) to inhabit all the Earth and also that man was in charge (as God's Vicegerents).

In Genesis we learn that after the Flood, mankind descended from Noah, his three sons and wives.

The only people who survived the Flood per the above, were Noah, his sons, and their wives. But somebody more, stood steadfastly by them who wouldn't let go. Satan had obviously been 'without work' for some time and was eagerly waiting for Noah's sons to get going, to go after them and their offspring, them (us) unknowing until this very day.

Something more that survived the Deluge was the genetic build-up of Noah and his family. To understand the importance of a gene, we need to know that the gene, with their respective DNA and Chromosomes, is the basic physical and functional unit of heredity. Thus, everything that had previously been created within man - both good and evil - continued being the same inherent detrimental building block of their offspring, mankind.

I say that Satan didn't have to begin from scratch. There was a 'trampoline' or 'springboard', which greatly facilitated Satan's work of deceit of the human beings.

The result of his many thousand years of arduous effort and work since the Creation to make mankind to fall – that began with the fall of Adam and Eve - can be observed everywhere around our planet, if one knows what to look for.

## 3.2 THE TOWER OF BABYLON. GOD CONFUSED THE ONLY LANGUAGE

After the Flood, the people populated the whole world (a small population at that time) and spoke only one language. As people wandered about, they arrived to Babylon and settled there.

They decided to build a city with a tower that was going to reach into the sky (to get close to God and thus become like him), so that we can live here and not have to spread all over.

At that point God came down to see the city and saw the tower that reached into the sky. HE didn't like what HE saw. They were one people speaking one language, who were intent on reaching into heaven. To avoid any further intentions of incursions into His Domain, HE gave them a multitude of new languages, in essence, one for each tribe. In the instant it took God to say 'Be' HE made it impossible for the people to understand each other. Then, God scattered them all over the World. And, the building of the Tower was stopped.

This was the second major punishment of God to mankind. God had made it impossible for mankind to keep together although they weren't destroyed.

The name of the city was Babylon, was where God mixed up the language of all the people. Therefrom comes the word 'babble' that has been made to mean confusion of words or language. In Swedish we say 'babla' (talk without meaning).

# 3.3 SODOM & GOMORRAH'S IMMORALITY CAUSED THEIR DESTRUCTION

From the Book of Genesis, we learn that Abraham was visited by two angels who told him that they were on their way to Sodom and Gomorrah against which there were terrible claims because of their sinful (immoral) ways.

To understand why they said this to Abraham, we need to go to the Jewish Bible, Book of Leviticus, wherein we learn that no man is to have sexual relations with another man, because God hates such a thing. It's also said that if a man has sexual relations with another man, it's something disgusting.

The same is valid for women having sex with each other.

The angels told Abraham that God was going to destroy the cities. Abraham pleaded with them not to kill the innocent people. After an extensive search however, none – except Lot - were found innocent, i.e., not being immoral.

The two angels went on to visit Lot - a son of a brother of Abraham, who lived in Sodom.

Lot was the only person in the whole City who had found pleasure in the eyes of God. Lot met the angels when they arrived at Sodom and invited them to his house.

We learn that during the night all men of Sodom both young and old surrounded the house. They called to Lot and asked, where the men where who came to stay with them where. They wanted them to come out, so they could have sex with them.

Lot offered them his virgin daughters, which the crowd refused. The men of Sodom then tried to get into the house by force. At that point the angels struck all the men outside with blindness, which prevented them from finding the door.

The angels told Lot that if he had any relatives living in the city to get them out of the city because God was going to destroy it. Lot went to see the men who were going to marry his daughters and told them to hurry up to get out of the city because God was going to destroy it.

But they laughed at him, thinking he was joking. At dawn, just before daybreak, the angels hurried Lot with wife and two daughters to leave the town.

They left, but, as we learn, Lot's wife looked back (something the angels had told them they were not allowed to do) and she was instantly turned into a pillar of salt. "The sun was rising when Lot reached the town of Soar (where he was going to take protection). At that moment, God rained fire with sulphur on the cities of Sodom and Gomorrah and the whole area, killing all the inhabitants and everything that lived on the land. Smoke raised like that of a huge furnace".

Both the Deluge and the destruction of Sodom and Gomorrah extensively the result of perversion (being gay and lesbian) of the then living people; the consequence of the temptations of Satan that people fell for; for which God destroyed them. In the above text of how God went about destroying these cities, we learn that HE rained fire with sulphur on the cities leaving everything desolate, never more to be inhabited.

The narrative provides evidence of how God put into practice His Punishment for the second time, of an unacceptable immoral mankind. The first time HE did it was with the Deluge.

The Question then arises, 'why have gay and lesbian people become 'approved' in today's societies?

The answer is simple. It is because Politicians looking at getting the Votes of those people have institutionalized the 'Rights' to be equal for the homosexual as for the heterosexual people.

From the above we learn that this is not approved by God! Be sure that the Politicians will be severely punished as well, when the Final Punishment takes place, as foretold.

# 3.4 GOD PUNISHED THE EGYPTIANS WITH TERRIBLE PLAGUES

IT OCCURRED BECAUSE THE PHARAOH RAMSES II REFUSED TO ALLOW THE ENSLAVED BADLY TREATED HEBREW PEOPLE TO LEAVE EGYPT.

The Story narrated in the Book of Exodus is truly miraculous. Therein God showed His awesome powers when HE punished the Egyptians with different kinds of horrible Plagues that hit and affected only them in many and different ways.

Incredibly, the Hebrew people who lived and worked intermingled with the Egyptians were untouched by the plagues.

God provides information in the Qur'an of what happened during that time as well. Among many things, God reveals that HE told Ramses II that his body would remain so that people could see it and thereby remember God. Ramses II body, which can be seen in a Museum in Cairo, Egypt, is amazingly well preserved.

I will not get in on that story that is remarkable, and real. For those interested, it serves to put in evidence the remarkable powers of the only living God. It is narrated in the Book of Exodus in the Bible and in Surah or Chapter 28 in the Qur'an.

God provides remarkable insights in the Qur'an of how HE first protected Baby Moses from Being killed by the soldiers of the ruling Pharaoh Seti I, the father of Ramses II, with whom Moses grew up, and later on, how HE guided His Prophet Moses, and gave him unique powers, such as to 'cut open' the Red Sea when he later on led the Jewish people away from Egypt.

In the same Chapter 28 in the Qur'an, God reveals that information of the destruction of prior pagan peoples was provided (by Him) 'as an eye opener', 'a guide', and how HE punished the Egyptians to be 'a reminder' for coming generations of what could (will) happen again.

In the Book of Revelation, what's revealed therein tells us, once what's written therein is understood, that God will use extraordinary punishments on a global scale affecting the Planet.

In the Jewish Bible, Book of Joshua (who God chose to continue the work of Moses to lead His people to the Promised Land), is told the Story of How God punished and eradicated all the pagan peoples (which are unacceptable to God) using and helping the Jewish people along their way from Egypt to the by God Promised Land, which HE had Promised to Abraham (Ibrahim) the Patriarch of the Peoples of God. His sons Isaac, the Patriarch of the Jews and Ishmael the Patriarch of Islam.

## 3.5 GOD'S IMPENDING FINAL PUNISHMENT OF MANKIND

Why I'm bringing up the matter of the final punishment in the context of God's previous punishments, is because of the punishments with which God punished the Egyptians - something that according to many accounts narrated in both the Jewish Bible and in the Qur'an - did happen.

What's so important about it is that the terrible things that occurred - according to the story - can be used to exemplify the punishment that God is about to begin to unleash on mankind. In the Book of Revelation are revealed punishments never before experienced that will be on a Global scale and therefore far worse that any before.

Because there exist the antecedents of how the Egyptians were punished, there's no doubt whatsoever that the punishments revealed in the Book of Revelation are going to happen. But not only that, looking at how our planet is behaving, I say that they are in the process of beginning to be carried out at any moment now, although nobody has understood any of that.

In the Book of Revelation, occurrences are described that are dreadful beyond imagination that resemble the punishments that God unlashed in Egypt some three thousand plus years ago when HE put Moses in command to get His Jewish People out from Egypt.

The story, described in the Book of Exodus in the TORAH, gives insight to the Awesome Might of God.

In the Book of Revelation Chapter 8, we learn that seven angels will blow horns that will set in motion terrible devastations. In Chapter 16, we learn that a loud voice spoke from the temple to seven angels, who were ordered to pour out on the earth the seven Bowls of the anger of God.

I suggest that to go in on the Internet and type in these Chapters to learn how our planet and mankind will be punished, extensively through the devastation of our planet.

The punishments that are revealed, will affect mankind in ways similar to how HE punished the Egyptian people and Pharaoh Ramses II when God drowned Him all his soldiers.

The stories seem to simply be stories, but I say, open your mind and try to put yourself into what's being narrated. It was horrific for the close to one-thousand Egyptian soldiers, when Pharaoh Ramses II forced them out in the opened path to chase the fleeing Jewish people, when God let the Red Sea, which HE had opened up for the fleeing Jews, fall over the Egyptians with all its force. Not one of the soldiers was able to save himself. Interestingly, rests of ancient chariots have recently been found in the Red Sea.

We find that the new Plagues – on hold for mankind - as I see it - will come upon those who remain alive when the end begins to close in; similar to the Egyptian plagues, but much worse.

The plagues – will affect and devastate extensive parts of Planet Earth as well as the remaining people who live in those areas! In the Book of Isaiah, we learn that God will strip the Earth bare and lay it waste, as it was before the creation.

You don't believe in this! Know that there isn't any escape out of any of it; and on '***the Day of Regret***', when it's going to be too late to change anything - you'll remember and will surely regret not having listened!

# CHAPTER 4

# REVELATIONS ABOUT AN EVIL 'RULER' AND A 'BEAST' AT THE END

These are revelations that were made about 'the ruler' and 'the beast' – a beast that God will make to emerge from the inside the earth - both of who – or maybe it's one and the same - are to appear at the End of Time, as follows.

The matter of 'the Ruler' – 'the beast' is addressed both in the Book of Daniel and in the Book of Revelation, as if they were the same, because of what's being said about them.

I'm attempting to address the subject that's exceptionally complicated and difficult to understand, because it's very nebulous in describing what will be taking place at the End of our Time, in the Sub-Chapters to follow.

## 4.1 THE BOOK OF DANIEL – ABOUT 'THE RULER'

Visions given to Daniel by the archangel Gabriel.

Daniel, a Prophet of God, was given visions about four mighty beasts different from each other that represented future empires. The archangel Gabriel appeared to Daniel and told him about them, but very especially about occurrences to take place at the End of Time. Daniel was told that the fourth beast, which was not like any of the others, fearsome, powerful and evil which was to appear at the End of Time.

I've spent countless amounts of hours to try to come to grips and understand the revelations that are related to the End of Time that Daniel was given, for a number of reasons. The most important was the way how future occurrences were described to happen.

We learn that the fourth beast represents a fourth empire that will be different from all previous empires that existed that will crush the whole earth.

What's happening in the Middle East, with all its violence and turmoil - as I understand - is setting the Scenario to put in place the last Empire, which will be evil beyond belief.

An evil man who is said to have no right to be king (Ruler) will appear unexpectedly and seize power by deceit. As it seems, as I have come to understand, it will be when, as it seems, the Tyrant Bashar al-Assad of Syria will be overthrown by somebody far eviller than he. Anyone opposing him will be swept away and wiped out.

The evil ruler will speak against God and oppress His people. He will work to change the laws and God's people will be under his power for three and a half years.

The Ruler, who is also mentioned in the Book of Revelation where it's called 'the beast', will be given authority over all nations the last years at the End.

It is said that the ruler will have a firm agreement with many nations for seven years. When half that time is past, he will put an end to sacrifices and offerings. *The Awful Horror* (which is mentioned in numerous prophecies as something terrible (Mark 13:17-29, Matthew

24:15-18, Luke 21:20-24) will be placed in the highest point of the Temple (of God) and will remain until the end.

The Ruler will bring war and destruction, which it's said that God put in place, which will carry on until the End, a time that was set by God.

Daniel saw 'the Heavenly Court' to sit in judgment. The Court took away the power of the Ruler - that had been given to him by God - and destroyed the Ruler completely.

Daniel tells us that he saw the fourth beast (the last empire) be destroyed and killed.

## 4.2 THE APOSTLE JOHN WHAT JESUS SAID, ABOUT 'THE RULER' AT THE END

These are mentions from the New Testament.

It is said that there will be a judging of mankind, at which time the evil ruler of the world will be disposed of.

Jesus told his Apostles that he wasn't going to continue talking with them, because *the ruler of the* world was going to appear.

Jesus said that the ruler of this world had been judged.

As we learned from the Qur'an, Satan was judged by God at the Creation of Adam because he disrespected Him, upon which he was cursed by God, Who gave him respite until 'the Day of Recompense' or Judgment Day.

# 4.3 THE APOSTLE MARK JESUS – ABOUT THE TIME AT THE END

From Jesus we learn that the days at the End will be worse than anything experienced before since God created the world.

I say that the war and holocaust caused by Hitler in the 1940s will seem small thing compared to what the evil Ruler is about to bring at the End.

Jesus also said that there will come a time when the sun will grow dark and the stars will fall from heaven.

We learn that the powers (the planets) in space will be driven from their courses. Read the prophecies of Merlin in chapter 5 that seem to confirm this. As I understand it, the planets in our Solar System will lose their current orbits.

Jesus said that no one knows when that day or hour (of the end) will happen, except God.

Today however we have a quite good approximation of when 'that time will come', by comparing all Prophecies and comparing them with current Reports of the effects of the Global Warming, how the Oceans are being affected – that's becoming more and more volatile, it's easy to assess that the End-of-Our-Time is 'knocking at our door'.

## 4.4 THE BOOK OF REVELATION BY JOHN FROM PATMOS

Before going forward, it's important to note that the revelations of Punishment to mankind given to John had already before been mentioned by the Prophets Isaiah in the Eighth Century BC and to Daniel in the Second Century BC, as detailed before.

Therefore, the revelations given to John of Patmos were not new. But they are unique because of the details of God's horror-filled Punishment of a wicked mankind – those who still remain at the End – who will be more and more decimated until the end.

The revelations provide information about terrible Punishments to be inflicted on mankind. As mentioned, one can compare them to the Plagues that God unleashed against the Egyptians in the time of Moses. But the difference is that those punishments affected Egypt and the Egyptians only. The ones revealed in the Book of Revelation will affect mankind globally.

The revelations given to John were described in no symbolic language, because John narrated what '*he thought he saw*' (to take place in the future, about two thousand Years away, which is now), using the words he knew. He saw things happening before his eyes, but much of it he in all certainty didn't understand and couldn't, therefore, describe properly.

The Revelations given to John in Chapters 4 through 19 are appalling because they describe in clear text the '*furious anger*' of the LORD God Almighty, when His Wrath is being poured out over the remainder of mankind, during the last few years of their existence - just prior to *the End of Our Time.*

The breaking of Seven Seals, described by John, open up different sufferings, representing the effects of what mankind has caused to itself (as the result of God's Karmic Divine LAW of 'Cause and Effect') (Revelations 6, 7 and 8).

The blowing of Seven Trumpets. The blowing of the trumpets opens up terrible torments (Revelation 8:6-13 and 9 and 11).

The pouring out of the Seven 'Bowls of God's Anger on the earth' by seven angels, which are said to be the last plagues of God's anger (Revelations 15:1 and 16).

All of the terrible punishments to affect mankind – are the effects of not obeying the Commandments of the Only Living God and for having abandoned His *Narrow Way*.

It's the reaping of the effects of the evil that mankind – each individual – has caused to one another and to Mother Earth.

By comparing texts in the Christian Bible with the Qur'an (Authored by God), we find numerous inconsistencies between them, showing that the original texts that had been given to John must have been altered.

# 4.5 THE EMERGENCE OF 'A BEAST' AT THE END AS REVEALED IN THE BOOK OF REVELATION AND THE QUR'AN

When I first read about the emergence of a beast in the Book of Revelation, I thought, one more of so many things that don't seem to make sense. But, when I found out that God mentions this in the Qur'an as well, I realized its appearance at the End is for real, as incredible as it sounds.

In the Qur'an we learn that the emergence of the Beast is a sign among major signs of the Hour (Day of Judgment). The beast will speak to people (unbelievers) who will worship it, telling them they did not believe with certainty in the Divine Signs.

The speaking beast will put in place evidence of the greatness of God, because beasts do not understand nor speak. The beast will have paranormal behaviour, proving to people that it is a great sign from God.

HE will make the beast to emerge at the end of time before the Day of Judgment. It will happen when mankind becomes corrupt, neglects His commandments and changes His religion.

# CHAPTER 5

# WHAT NON-SCRIPTURE PROPHET 'SEERS' HAVE SAID

### COMPLEMENTING GOD'S ANCIENT PROPHECIES MAKING THEM UNDERSTANDABLE

In the following, I'm providing the words of a few individuals, who I call '*Seers*'. But, before going further, I want to state that I believe it's impossible that any of them could 'see' future occurrences by themselves. The only explanation is that God gave them '*the faculty to see our future*', to tell us about it! There's absolutely no other way.

The future occurrences that these people reported are important because they provide - as I've found - information that complements what God foretold about in His ancient Prophecies, especially those in the Jewish Bible and in the Book of Revelation.

In addition, they help to establish a reasonably exact time frame for when the End of Time will take place, something that the ancient prophecies don't.

I found this, when I compiled all the prophecies, analysing and comparing them between each other. In the following, we shall learn what those 'Seers' said of the remarkable future occurrences – mostly terrifying ones - they were given to 'see'.

In Chapter 6, a Chart shows the result of my compilation.

## 5.1 THE UNPARALLELED 'PROPHECIES' OF AMERICAN 'SEER' EDGAR CAYCE

The prophecies of famous American Edgar Cayce, often called '*the American Sleeping Prophet*', are unparalleled for a number of reasons, as we shall find out in the following!

Edgar Cayce (1877 – 1945) - often also called '*the other Nostradamus*' - I view as one of the most amazing and insightful prophet-like 'seer' of all times. Type in his name on the Internet to find how much Edgar Cayce did to help people in so many different ways using his unique 'powers' too 'see'.

Cayce used to lie down and set himself in trance. While in trance he was asked all kinds of questions of interest to the individual posing the question. Cayce reached out (he said) into the spiritual realm (past and future), bringing in information on so many different subjects that it was simply remarkable.

A secretary took shorthand notes of everything Cayce said. There exists an array of books about him and his revelations, which provide awesome insights of him.

Cayce said that the Earth *was (is)* going to go through severe climate changes. The result would be cataclysmic movements and changes of the Continents, including the devastation of the North American Continent, to take place in our time.

It is important to know that Cayce was known for his amazing assertiveness in a multitude of very varying subjects, completely unrelated to the End-of-Time Prophecies. He never failed about anything he said.

Cayce died on January 3, 1945 (the date that he had mentioned he would die). At that moment nobody had an idea or knowledge of the effects of the current Global Warming of the Atmosphere – that has extensively been caused by man.

Nothing was known about how the warmed up and poisonous effects of the Atmosphere would affect the Oceans; and how that, in turn, would cause the melting of the vast ice-sheets in Antarctica and Greenland. From where did he get that insight?

This is a strong indication that tells us that yes Cayce could reach out and 'see' into the unseen realms of our future.

Edgar Cayce foretold many coming occurrences. He mentioned about natural disasters, including Hurricane Katrina and the earthquake in Japan to be in 2010 or 2011.

In 1934, some years before it happened, Cayce predicted the beginning and end of World War II. He predicted the end of Communism, and that Russia would be born again (as it's doing).

He predicted a shift on Planet Earth's Rotation axis to occur in 2011. The earthquake in Japan affected the earth's axis on Friday, March 2011, very minimally, but it was affected, as it also was by the earthquake in Sumatra.

Cayce referred to Atlantis some 700 times in his readings over many years. The 'sleeping prophet' placed the sunken landmass between the Gulf of Mexico and the Mediterranean. He revealed that the lost continent was destroyed by a series of natural cataclysms that took place between twelve-thousand and seventeen-thousand years ago, for which he said, the evil behaviour of man, made it to happen.

Cayce made numerous revelations of cataclysmic occurrences that would take place very soon, which would lead to the devastation of our planet.

You can go in on the Internet and type in for instance 'what *Cayce said about the End*' or anything. Following Cayce's 'revelations' about the devastation of the North American Continent, a map was drawn showing what it will look like. It's also found on the Internet.

In the following some of the Catastrophic Earth changes mentioned by Cayce that can also be found on the Internet, just about to begin to devastate our planet, as the result of the accelerating effects of the Global Warming.

He said that the earth will be broken up in many places. The American West Coast including Los Angeles and San Francisco will undergo widespread destruction. New York State's East Coast and New York City itself will disappear. (Maybe as the result of a potential Mega Tsunami from a Canary Islands Volcano named Cumbre Vieja?)

Europe will be changed. The Scandinavian Countries will disappear in just one moment, as will Japan.

Cayce also mentioned that our planet will tilt over so that where there's now cold climate it'll become warm (and vice versa of course).

I could go on and on. If you want to know more, you can find on the Internet what more Cayce said.

Cayce mentioned that '*There will come a time when the sun will be darkened, which* clearly compares to God's revelations in scriptures, to which I made reference.

Quite amazingly, Cayce mentioned that there will be an increase in volcanic activity around the Pacific Rim. (Increased volcanic activity clearly will cause '*the sun to be darkened*'.)

I contend that the occurrences mentioned by Cayce are imminently close to begin to happen because they are the result of the effects of the Global Warming on the Oceans!

If we realize that Cayce never failed on any of his many revelations, then missing out on the year becomes unimportant because it's simply a matter of time. Instead '*the list of all the destruction he piled up that he said will happen*', is still '*on course to happen*'.

And, based on all the Articles related to the Effects of the Global Warming on the Oceans, being published on the Internet on an almost daily base, it's becoming more and more evident that we are on a course that's accelerating towards the by Cayce described occurrences of devastation.

Cayce missed out on the year, for the reason stated by Jesus, who said, *that No one knows when that day and hour will take place, God alone knows!*

## 5.2 THE ANCIENT PROPHECIES OF THE AMERICAN HOPI INDIANS

Many years ago, I learned about the American Hopi Indians and their unique ancient Prophecies. They are considered one of the oldest living cultures in the world, with their history stretching back thousands of years. The Hopi Tribe is a sovereign nation located in north-eastern Arizona. Their reservation is made up of 12 villages on three mesas. Since time long lost the Hopi people have lived there and have maintained their sacred covenant with Maasaw, also called the Great Spirit (God), to live as peaceful and humble farmers respectful of the land and its resources.

In accordance to Hopi oral tradition, the Great Spirit revealed to them that white men would come and take their land and try to lead them into evil ways. They were told that despite of all the pressures against them by the white men, they must hold to their ancient religion and their land, always without violence. If they succeeded, the Great Spirit promised that their people and their land would be a centre from which the True Spirit would be reawakened.

Over the centuries the Hopi have survived as a tribe, although strongly decimated, and have managed to retain their culture, language and religion despite at times strong pressures and bad treatment from the outside world (the American Governments).

Early on the Hopi were told of two, what they call 'great shakings' (World Wars I and II) that would occur. They were told about the mushroom that would be seen in the sky (the A-bomb) as the end of time got closer.

According to Hopi prophecy there will be a World War III that will be ignited somewhere in the east. The United States will be destroyed by 'gourds of ashes' falling to the ground, boiling the rivers and burning the earth, where grass won't grow for many years, causing diseases that medicines can't cure. Sounds like the effects of the Atomic Bomb.

This Prophecy coincides extensively with revelations written in Chapters 8, 9 and 16, in the Book of Revelation.

The Continental United States, which they call '*Turtle Island*', will destroy itself from within as the result of its way of increasingly living unspiritual ('pastime') lives.

The Hopi say that our condition is that of '*a society out of balance…a state of life that calls for another way of living.*'

The Hopi also prophesied that '*Turtle Island*' would turn over two or three times. As a result, they were told that '*the oceans would join hands with the sky*', which sounds as Tsunamis of unimaginable height, as mentioned elsewhere.

Because of how interesting the Hopi Prophecies are, my spouse and I drove to Arizona and visited them during a few years ago. My observation is that the Hopi are the only Prophets who are alive and can talk about revelations of the future that '*The Great Spirit*', gave them long time ago.

When talking about Prophecies with our Hopi-guide he said, "*We will soon have ocean-front to the Pacific Ocean.*" And I know he wasn't joking!

In this regard, I suggest to go in on the Internet and take a look at Cayce's map mentioned in the previous sub-Chapter. With our guide, we visited the Prophecy Rock that narrates the story of mankind from the beginning to its end, which he explained.

It goes from the beginning of time to the End of the World. To see it, please visit the following link.

http://www.viewzone.com/hopi.prophecy.html

# 5.3 IRISH BISHOP MALACHI'S AWESOME PROPHECY OF THE POPES

An interesting Prophecy that provides information relative to '*the time of the end*' – as I've found - is the one of Irish Bishop Malachi from Ireland (1094 – 1148). It is so because it provides '*a small window of time*' for when the End is to happen, take or give a few years.

There exist question-marks about the veracity of this Prophecy, and that it may be some kind of hoax. But, after reading it over and over, I've come to the conclusion that there's a high probability that it's true, reason to bring it in. This is so because his Prophecies of especially the most recent Popes have been exacting, and must therefore be viewed as believable. I say that he who lives shall see. It's an interesting Prophecy anyhow, worth the while to have in mind.

The story goes that Bishop Malachi was visiting with Pope Innocent II in Rome in the year 1139 when the bishop received a vision of all the future popes – to be as many as 112 – from that day *and until Judgment Day*. He gave a written account of his vision to the Pope that was kept secret and wasn't discovered in the Vatican archives until in 1590.

Despite the fact that there have been many debates related to the prophecies, they gained a large following over the last few years for their remarkable accuracy in predicting some attributes of recent popes, including Benedict XVI, the former and next to last (111$^{th}$) Pope, who relinquished his position.

As to the last pope, the current one, Francis, the Prophecy reads that he would take the name Peter the Roman, which as we know he didn't.

The Prophecy declares that '*The 112$^{th}$ pope (irrelevant of his name), will feed his flock amid many tribulations, after which the seven-hilled City* (Rome – seat of the Vatican) *will be destroyed and the Great Judge* (the Only Living God), *will judge the people* (mankind) *at The End* (on Judgment Day).'

Since Malachi's prophecies accurately described the previous three pontiffs, this can only mean that the end is close at hand.

The substance of the vision is no problem since it resembles that of the Book of Revelation in the Bible (read Chapters 17 and 18). The issue is one of chronology.

Is then Judgment Day at hand? It certainly looks that way.

I contend that Francis in all probability wanted to avoid his 'destiny' by adopting a different name. Alternatively, maybe he simply wanted to avoid publicity.

Whatever the case I say that avoiding the name, doesn't avoid being the 112th Pope or his destiny.

## 5.4 THE ASTONISHING PROPHECIES OF UNKNOWN ITALIAN PROPHET

Gerolamo Tovazzo, unknown to most, was born in northern Italy 1686 and died in Rome 1769. In his book, "*The Prophetic Garden*", Tovazzo provided among other, some of the most remarkable prophecies that relate to the time of the End of the World (our planet). Follow, some of the things that he said.

*Degenerate* (immoral, corrupt, perverted, decadent, etc) *Rome will end in the ashes.*" (This is an amazing Prophecy that goes 'Hand-in-hand' with what was revealed to John in Rev 18:9.)

*When our time is at its end, Christians (will realize* that they) *are pagans.*

*The resurgence of faith will not come from rotten Rome, but from the East* (in all probability meaning 'Islam').

*Their faith* (of Christians) *will be on the money and in the power; corruption and violence will triumph.*

When the angel's shadow passes; the gates of the cemeteries will be opened. A tremendous thunder, a whirl; and everything will pass fast."

Many lands will shake and the mountains will disappear."

The seas will go mad (because of Mega Tsunamis, which will be caused when Tectonic Plates crash into each other or separate.)

A deep plough will turn the lands of the world (when Planet Earth flips over) making them infertile.

***The earth will finally rest in peace!***

## 5.5 THE MIND-BLOWING PROPHECIES OF MERLIN – THE WIZARD

Merlin, generally known as the Wizard and wise man in Arthurian legend of the middle-Ages has been linked with individuals in ancient Celtic mythology, and especially with the Welsh 'Myrddin'.

The timeframe for when the Prophecies were made isn't known, but it's thought that there were several individuals that were made into one character, namely the enigmatic wizard, adviser and guide of King Arthur, Merlin.

To my knowledge, Merlin has never been mentioned to be a Prophet. However, the awesome "*Last Day Prophesies*" ascribed to him, means that one of the characters must have possessed the gift to actually 'see' what will happen in the future.

The prophecies ascribed to Merlin, as we shall find in the following are 'out of this World', especially in regards to what he said about the planets of our solar system.

He indicated that the cult of religion (Christianity) will be destroyed completely (at the end). He said that the ruins of the (Christian) churches shall be visible to everybody. These are revelations that Merlin can only have obtained from God.

Men will become drunk with the wine which is offered to them (surely Satan has to do with this). They will turn their back on Heaven (God) and fix their eyes on the Earth (materialism).

The seas shall rise in a split second of an eye (Tsunamis).

The dust of the elders (the bodies) shall be restored (when every person shall be resurrected to stand Trial)

The river Thames overflows and will submerge nearby towns. It will join itself to the springs of Celebes (I haven't been able to find what is meant by this), filled as they are to the very rim with wickedness and deceit.

The harvest will dry up through the anger of the stars and all moisture from the sky will cease.

What Merlin said about the planets is astounding.

Before the amber glow of Mercury, the bright light of the sun shall become dim and strike horror in those who witness it. Mercury shall overrun its orbit (abandoning it).

The stars (rather the planets of our solar system) will avert their gaze and alter their accustomed course (orbits).

Jupiter shall abandon its preordained path and Venus will desert its appointed circuit.

Merlin said about Saturn that it will pour down an acid-like precipitation, killing mortal men as it was made with a curved sickle.

Sounds like the fulfilment of punishments described in the Book of Revelation.

It also sounds to be the disintegration of our Solar System.

## 5.6 THE TERRIFYING PROPHECIES OF NOSTRADAMUS

Nostradamus, 1503 to 1566, a French scientist, alchemist and many things more, is probably the best known 'Seer' worldwide, comparable only maybe to the "Other Nostradamus", Edgar Cayce and to some extent to the biblical John from Patmos, who was given the 'Revelations of the End of Time'.

In the Book of Revelation in the Christian Bible, we learn that John was taken by angels of God, to see (in visions) the things that would take place in the future, at the end of time.

The same is valid for the Prophecies described in the Book of Daniel in the Bible. This tells us that all things are known by God, Who is All-Knowing, All-Seeing, All-Wise. We see it as future things to come, while God saw our future current without any time-constraint.

I'm convinced that Nostradamus didn't make any, what we call 'predictions' and that he had the gift of 'seeing the future', as also John from Patmos, and Daniel in the Old Testament, and as I also believe was the case with Edgar Cayce, as mentioned.

Nostradamus had to avoid providing clear descriptions of what he had 'seen' because he feared the Inquisition of that time. They would have declared a witch and burned him to death, had they learned about his abilities.

In all probability, many of the things he saw couldn't anyhow be described by him with words of his time. How would he have described today's war-machines, such as war-tanks, submarines, airplanes and airplane carriers, etcetera?

In order to avoid mass-hysteria, Nostradamus was probably not either allowed by God to tell in clear words the horrible things he was given to see of future cataclysmic occurrences!

Some of his Quatrains (four-line verses) provide horrific glimpses related to the End of our world (our Planet) and of mankind, such as the coming of a foretold beast, the third and last World-War now in most probability in the making, the use of what must have been atomic bombs that he obviously couldn't describe what they were.

Nostradamus mentioned the inversion of the Poles (rather the tipping of Planet Earth, as the rotation axis seeks a new balanced position) and much more. Something that would lead to the devastation of Planet Earth (as described by Edgar Cayce) and of mankind.

This is clearly the result of the collective accumulated evil doings of mankind that are in the process of putting in place devastation through natural disasters; such as powerful earthquakes and the ensuing tsunamis, and volcano eruptions. In addition to this, there will be atomic bombs and other weapons of mass destruction.

From the Christian Bible we learn that a final war is to take place at Armageddon. Whatever that is, it will be a fight between good and evil. To give an idea of its consequences, Nostradamus wrote the following, one of his very last Quatrains (Number 6-81 from 1557).

*"Tears cries, and laments, howls, terror.*
*Inhuman heart, cruel, black, and making one*
*shudder with fear. Blood to be shed,*
*hunger for bread and cheese, to none mercy."*

The Quatrain gives the idea of how horrible things will become in that last years with, as he wrote, *'mercy to none'*.

Satan knows that he is nearing the end of his time, the Day of Resurrection until when God gave Satan respite after HE was disobeyed, when Satan will go to hell. Because Satan (and his army) knows his time is nearing the end, he's working 'overtime' to take with him as many as he can of mankind - down the pit of Hell! I say that there will not be many left on the *'Narrow Way'* of God after Satan is finished misleading mankind.

Nostradamus appears to have predicted natural disaster across the United States. One area of special concern that he seems to have mentioned must have to do, as I see it with the fault lines of San Andrea and San Jacinto just outside Los Angeles. Then there's the Cascadian Subduction zone north thereof that is of great concern to scientists. All three have been said to be overdue to cause mayor catastrophic earthquakes.

What Nostradamus said, '*An earthquake shall concern particularly the western area of the United States. Its power,* (to shake the whole planet) *shall be felt in lands throughout the world.*'

Let's recall what Cayce said about '*America's West Coast including Los Angeles and San Francisco will undergo widespread destruction*', and will be eliminated from the map.

Those of you who are interested can go in on the Internet to see what 'Cayce's *map of a future – very different - Continental United States*' will look like.

## 5.7 THE CHINESE I-CHIN ORACLE

The 5000-year-old I-Chin Oracle has the same end date for what many thought would be the End of the World (of our planet). The highs and lows of the I-Chin time-line graph have accurately coincided with several great historical occurrences.

What's remarkable is that its end-date is the same as that of the Maya calendar, December 21, 2012. It can't be a coincidence. But what is then their message?

## 5.8 THE INTRIGUING MAYA CALENDAR

The Mayan Calendar is intriguing for many reasons. It's date on December 21, 2012, was when many thought to be the End of the World (of our planet). As the result of what I had learned from the Prophecies of God, I knew that that couldn't be the case. As we know, nothing happened, at least nothing visible.

What the Maya Calendar signalled was not the End of something. It was, I believe, the beginning of a new very short epoch, when mankind transitioned into its (our) last – very short time-period – that was never before - and will never be again.

# CHAPTER 6

# PROPHECIES (PROPHETS AND THEIR PROPHECIES – SUMMARIZED) of Our Unfortunate Destiny - Summarized in One Chart!

The Details in the Slide are described in detail & discussed throughout the Book.

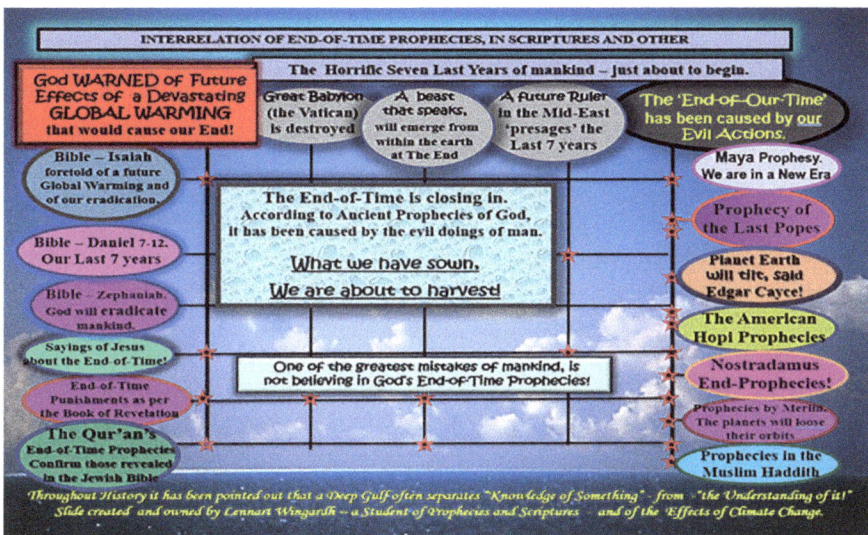

INTERRELATION OF END-OF-TIME PROPHECIES, IN SCRIPTURES AND OTHER

The Horrific Seven Last Years of mankind – just about to begin.

God WARNED of Future Effects of a Devastating GLOBAL WARMING that would cause our End!

Great Babylon (the Vatican) is destroyed

A beast that speaks, will emerge from within the earth at The End

A future Ruler in the Mid-East 'presages' the Last 7 years

The 'End-of-Our-Time' has been caused by our Evil Actions.

Bible – Isaiah foretold of a future Global Warming and of our eradication.

Maya Prophesy. We are in a New Era

Bible – Daniel 7-12. Our Last 7 years

The End-of-Time is closing in. According to Ancient Prophecies of God, it has been caused by the evil doings of man.

What we have sown,

We are about to harvest!

Prophecy of the Last Popes

Planet Earth will tilt, said Edgar Cayce!

Bible – Zephaniah. God will eradicate mankind.

Sayings of Jesus about the End-of-Time!

End-of-Time Punishments as per the Book of Revelation

The American Hopi Prophecies

One of the greatest mistakes of mankind, is not believing in God's End-of-Time Prophecies!

Nostradamus End-Prophecies!

Prophecies by Merlin. The planets will loose their orbits

The Qur'an's End-of-Time Prophecies Confirm those revealed in the Jewish Bible

Prophecies in the Muslim Haddith

Throughout History it has been pointed out that a Deep Gulf often separates "Knowledge of Something" - from "the Understanding of it!" Slide created and owned by Lennart Wingardh – a Student of Prophecies and Scriptures – and of the Effects of Climate Change.

In this Chart, Prophecies have been brought together to show how they interrelate.

## The two major events in the Chart

1. The red square in the left upper corner relates to Prophecies wherein God warned about the future *"Effects of today's Global Warming"*, which Nobody ever understood!

2. The oblong figure with the yellow text in the upper right corner. We observe that practically all Prophecies – *wherein God foretold what would happen* - 'point to' the 'End-of-Time'.

## CHAPTER 7
# THE DAY OF RESURRECTION IS FOLLOWED BY JUDGMENT DAY

In the Qur'an, the only Book that, as we know, God (called Allah in Arabic) ever authored, HE dedicated lots of space in the last Chapters to reveal what will occur during and immediately after the 'tipping' of our planet. That will be 'it' as the result of the eradication of all human and animal life, which was foretold by God, for the first time – as mentioned - through His Prophet Isaiah, close to Two-thousand-Eight-hundred years ago.

HE expressed it the clearest through His Prophet Zephaniah wherein it's written that God *said that HE was going to destroy everything on (planet) earth, mankind and animals and leave no survivors.* Mankind will be gone all of the sudden and forever.

In the following a few of the many mentions that God has provided in the Qur'an about the dreadful matters that are imminently close to take place, which are - 'caused' to occur, by the man-made Global Warming.

God deals with and explains these matters with great detail in the Qur'an, as warnings to all human beings about what is in an advanced process to happen to everybody.

HE has revealed that each of us shall receive a recompense or reward, entirely dependent on what we did with our lives while here on earth - which HE says - HE gave to us to do something with, and that we believe in Him – in our hearts - that HE is '*the Only Living God*' and obey His Commands! (I want to refer to what HE said through His Prophet Isaiah 29:13 in this regard)

After the End of our earthly life comes the Resurrection of the by God re-established bodies with their souls.

Every human being (*nobody excluded through a man-invented inexistent 'rapture' that Christians have been made to believe in*) will be taken by our respective assigned guardian angel to stand trial in front of God on the Day of Judgment.

It's an interesting but also most terrifying reading, for all those (most of us) who won't make it to 'The Kingdom of God'.

Each one of us will be given our respective '*Book of Deeds*'.

In Qur'an 84:11 we learn that those who are given their respective book from behind their backs in the left hand, the largest group by far - most of mankind – standing to the left of the Judge, know they're lost, and will desire they were dead.

A second group, no more than a few percent who are given their '*Book of Deeds*' in their right hand will stand to the right of the Great Judge, looking happy.

A Third, very small group will stand in front of the Great Judge with their '*Book of Deeds*' in the right hand – looking very happy. This very small - secluded group - are those in whom the Lord has found pleasure.

To which group will you belong?

What will happen from this moment and until the end?

In the next Chapter 8, the last, we shall learn about the things that will take place when our Planet Earth begins to feel the increasing impacts of the destructive Effects of the man-made Global Warming!

# THE EFFECTS OF THE GLOBAL WARMING ON PLANET EARTH

This Chapter, to which I've referred numerous times, as its title indicates, is about the effects of the Global Warming also known as Climate Change, how it's affecting our planet.

As we've learned, God, for the first time - as far back as close to twenty-eight hundred years ago – issued Prophecies that were intended as warnings of extreme climate changes that would cause calamities of great consequence to our planet. It would occur in a distant future, severely affecting our planet's atmosphere, HE warned.

In this Chapter we shall examine the Effects of the current Global Warming as we read mostly every day about how it's proceeding in articles on the Internet covering its many facets.

The purpose is to bring what's happening today to our planet - into the context of the revelations of God in the Ancient Prophecies in Scriptures as well as in numerous '*non-scripture*' ones described in Chapter 5.

This is made in an effort to compare 'ancient prophecies' and 'current occurrences' affecting our planet - side-by-side - as apples-to-apples.

Many years ago, I discovered that the prophecies of God were warnings about effects to be caused to our planet by the Global warming.

Because of this, I began to follow the 'tons' of articles on this subject that flood the internet, with the Goal in mind to understand the interrelation that seemed to me existed between them and the ancient prophecies of God.

What soon became very clear to me was that the only thing that could cause a cataclysmic change to our planet was a redistribution of waters of the Oceans. They're the only 'Element' – 70 % of our planet's surface - that could cause the colossal changes and devastation to our planet that God described in His prophecies.

From reading the prophecies over and over, and making numerous compilations between them all, it became clear to me what it was that was in the process of taking place.

This Chapter will take us through what it's all about.

# 8.1 GOD FORTOLD OF A FUTURE DESTRUCTIVE GLOBAL WARMING

We shall find that God's ancient prophecies – wherein HE revealed *'what HE saw would happen in a distant Future'* without the least doubt referred to the effects of today's man-made Global Warming that would affect the atmosphere.

The atmosphere in turn – as we've been learning from the many reports on the internet – has severely affected the Oceans. This is a strongly 'fluctuating *element*' – covering two thirds of the surface of Planet Earth - that has the potential to devastate our planet.

I'll be repeating myself of things I mentioned before to clearly establish that God foretold about our demise! At issue is to determine what it is that's in the process of taking place and how it is and will continue affecting our planet.

Before continuing I state again that what God foretold about our future - every word HE pronounced - is inalterable and is on due course to be fulfilled. Of acute importance for mankind are His many Prophecies of disaster that would (in the process to) affect Planet Earth, sending it and us into oblivion!

God foretold about man-made occurrences (in other words, phenomena that man would cause – resulting from its insatiable greed) - that would produce appalling upheavals to our planet.

As mentioned before, God could (can) *'see'* occurrences happening in what we call *'the future'* (which we humans obviously can't) such as the fateful destiny of mankind and the devastation of our Planet Earth, or anything!

Revelations of our future that God made through a host of different so-called prophets and other individuals, as those described in Chapter 5, are all coming together now in our time.

Unfortunately for us, mankind, the Jewish people didn't share the teachings that God had given to them, as HE ordered them to do - according to what's written in the Qur'an 3:187-189 – keeping the knowledge for themselves.

Scientists and politicians or anybody don't want to accept the fact that today's Global Warming - or rather the multiple destructive ripple effects it's producing – was foretold by God thousands of years ago.

But yes, God saw it happening - as we learned before - and time after time HE gave His prophets Visions about it. Unfortunately, they were never able to adequately understand and describe what was going on in the Visions. I believe that since they didn't understand any of it, they didn't put in any effort into trying to understand what it was all about.

As God revealed, as described before, because of their lack of interest, HE withheld from them the knowledge of it, as HE declared, as strange as it may sound. On the other hand, the people of today's modern era don't believe in any of that, such as what Bishop Shelby wrote in his book '*The Sins of Scripture*' - and of course – the World's Earth Science community.

I made numerous attempts to contact Scientists, including at Harvard to discuss my findings, but they didn't respond to my letters. When I called Professor Jerry Mitrovica, he answered the phone, but told me he didn't have time to see me.

As we've learned, God's Prophets were unable to understand and adequately describe what they had been shown. I've concluded that the probable reason why they couldn't understand was because they had no idea that our planet, earth as God called it, was a round sphere that rotates around itself, and around the sun.

Still in the year 1490AD, when Columbus was planning his voyage to what he thought was the West Indies, he was initially unable to man his three ships. And that was because of the then prevailing belief that the earth was flat.

Since Columbus destiny was unknown, it was thought that the ships would reach a point at the end of the ocean where they could fall over the edge never to return home. How he resolved the subject matter is another story.

The idea that the earth was flat in all probability also led to what's said in Isaiah 11:12 and Revelation 7:1 of "*The Four Corners of the earth.*"

Going back to our subject, the obvious question is why it matters to know whether the earth was flat or round. I've found it to be a matter of great consequence as we shall find out.

Since God in His revelations of our planet God used the word 'earth', nothing else, it was impossible to get an idea of what the earth looked like.

The 'Key' to understanding what is about to happen with our planet any day soon - as we reach the End-of-Time - was foretold by God, as mentioned before.

In several End-of-Time prophecies it was said that '*the stars would fall down to the earth and that the sky would look like a scroll that's being rolled up*'. We need to examine what it is that really shall happen, as we continue.

Astronomy was one of my best subjects in school and I learned that the tiny stars are gigantic suns, which are '*light years*' away. It's therefore impossible - as we realize - that they could fall down on Planet Earth all at once since it would take them light-years to reach us.

Therefore, what the Prophets saw taking place in the visions presented to them by God was something very different.

To the Prophets, the tiny stars in the skies were just that '*tiny stars*'. They had not the slightest idea that they were '*distant gigantic suns that were light years away*'.

And, we can be sure that they had no idea of '*light years*'. What God showed that looked like falling stars and the sky that disappeared as a scroll being rolled up, will be discussed, as we continue.

How could anything like that happen? If I had tried to understand and explain what was happening some forty-plus years ago, I wouldn't have been able to do it, because there weren't yet any signs of significance - as there are now - of the effects of the current Global Warming.

Today, with the effects of the Global Warming or Climate Change in an increasingly accelerating process of melting so many glaciers it's an entirely different story. Now, as the result – of what's going on – I can explain God's ancient End-of-Time Prophecies.

God didn't want that what was to happen in our destructive future to be comprehended until at the End-of-Our-Time. His prophecies about the end – were to be kept secret until the time when God would make them 'come to life'.

In Daniel 12:10, the angel told Daniel that some people would be purified (at the end), while those who were wicked (the great majority of mankind) will not understand and would go on being wicked. Only those (a few) who were (are) wise will understand (the revelations of God).

## 8.2 THE GLOBAL WARMING - PICTURES TELL MORE THAN WORDS

Pictures tell more than words, so before taking off on our journey, I'm providing pictures that give an idea of what it's all about. In other words, the idea is to show how our planet is changing, very rapidly. Look at these colossal pieces of ice collapsing and melting.

*Credit: Ian Phillips, Australian Antarctic Division.*

What you see is ice calving (breaking) off from an ice shelf in West Antarctica. The problem with this is that it's an occurrence that's in the process of growing exponentially, with nothing to stop it from continuing to happen, or even to make its accelerating pace to slow down.

Fast-draining lakes threaten vulnerable Greenland ice sheet. Reports on the Internet based on NASA Satellite measurements tell us that the Greenland Ice-sheet is melting by far, faster that than anybody expected it to do.

Greenland's ice sheet, the second largest on Earth, appears to be perfectly still, but is it? GISP refers to a main site of the **Greenland Ice Sheet Project**, with a 3 kilometre's high ice core (about 2 Miles) that's melting at an ever-increasing speed, far faster than thought, in accordance to the NASA Satellite measurements (per August 2019). From

https://www.upi.com/Science_News/2018/03/14/Fast-draining-lakes-threaten-vulnerable-Greenland-ice-sheet/2321521030289/

March 14, 2018 (UPI). Scientists study large fractures in Greenland's ice sheet produced by chain-reaction melting events. Photo by Samuel Doyle/Cambridge University

A quarter century ago, Greenland's ice sheet was stable, or so it was thought. Today, it's losing millions of metric tons of ice every day. As Greenland's ice melt accelerates, sea levels rise, scientists warn.

Scientists shared their analysis of the drainage dynamics on Greenland's ice sheet in a paper published on March 2018, in the journal Nature Communications.

The study's authors say only a sharp reduction in greenhouse gas emissions can ensure Greenland's ice sheet doesn't become completely destabilized.

Svalbard's (Norway) enormous glaciers are in full retreat in the Arctic.

The Svalbard's, that belong to Norway, are a group of islands in the Arctic Ocean. Why they are of interest is because of the many large Glaciers that cover them that are in full retreat, thus adding to the melt-waters of mainly Greenland and Iceland that are full filling the Oceans. Unfortunately, I don't know the origin of this Photo, to give the corresponding Credit.

How loss of Arctic Sea ice further fuels global warming.. By Frank Jordans - The Associated Press

http://www.seattletimes.com/nation-world/how-loss-of-arctic-sea-ice-further-fuels-global-warming/

Sea ice melts away on the Franklin Strait along the Northwest Passage in the Canadian Arctic Archipelago. Because of climate change, more sea ice is being lost each summer than is being replenished during the winter. (AP Photo/David Goldman).

Less sea ice coverage means that less sunlight will be reflected off the dark surface of the ocean, which means that the Ocean water will absorb more heat, further fuelling Global Warming.

As you surely have realized by now, the Destiny of our Planet is tightly intertwined with the melt-waters from the melting vast ice sheets in mainly the Antarctic Continent and in Greenland.

And that's so because the accelerating unstoppable ice-melt is causing a growing massive re-distribution of the weight of Planet Earth – that, in turn, is causing a continually increasing imbalance. The increasing imbalance, in turn, affects the rotation axis that's becoming more and more unstable.

How do we stop it from continuing to happen? The really bad news is that there's nothing that can stop it from keeping on destabilizing, something that's occurring faster and faster.

## 8.3 'PLAYING DUMB' ON CLIMATE CHANGE – A SCIENTIST SAID

This heading no doubt sounds strange, doesn't it? So why do I bring it up? I will immediately mention who said it, and the circumstances around it.

I say that the Earth Scientists distancing from Religion is as a major offence to God, since it means that they – themselves unknowing - rejected His teachings. It is so because the Jewish Religion – its Bible - embraces the prophecies of God – wherein HE, through them - foretold what would happen to our planet and to mankind.

I learned of the Earth Scientists adversity to religion in an article by Harvard's Professor Naomi Oreskes. In the Article, titled *"Playing Dumb on Climate Change"*, she said, *"Even as scientists consciously reject religion as a basis of natural knowledge, they.....*" Also, even if these Scientists don't realize it, they have committed a great offence against God for rejecting His Revelations.

Knowing what I've learned from my research on the Prophecies of God, I became shocked when I read it. You can find the Article on the Link below. I found that by simply entering *playing-dumb-on-climate-change* it immediately came up in my Yahoo server.

I view it as a human tragedy of format. Well, nothing could change our Destiny, which we humans architected.

Our conventional way of thinking about God is in our way. HE, the Only Living God is a Spiritual Being – so extraordinarily unique – that it's impossible for us to comprehend His Greatness.

His Powers that allow Him to create what HE wills with His Mind - are Infinite – far beyond our limited capacity to understand.

Earth Scientists seem to believe that by reducing the Emissions, damage to the Atmosphere can be curtailed. Nothing could be farther from the truth. If the Earth Science Community had been humble and taken away their *'we reject religion'* attitude and read the revelations of God in the Jewish Bible (and in the Qur'an) as mentioned above, they would have had a different understanding and criteria of the matters of Climate Change and would have avoided *'Playing Dumb'*.

If you paid attention to what I mentioned before, you know by now that nothing we do can change the damage already inflicted to the Oceans!

If they had paid attention to what God said in the Jewish Bible, the Earth Scientists at Harvard and all other Universities would have understood that nothing can be done to reverse any of what God foretold would occur.

I want to repeat that this is so, so we have in mind that what God revealed – '*was what HE saw taking place in the future*' – which was the product of our doings – not of God!

One could say that HE was watching and provided warnings about what HE saw would take place in our future.

God told His prophets about this matter and I strongly believe that what he told them was that there was no hope whatsoever to prevent our self-inflicted future devastation from happening; as we've learned from the foregoing.

Planet Earth is positioned on a '*path*' that's leading to its auto-destruction. It's so because '*the mechanism*' to make it happen is '*securely in place*' in the depths of the Oceans.

The '*Start button*' is waiting to be depressed, something that will happen at the occurrence of a foretold event as revealed in the Book of Daniel in the Jewish Bible, to occur at any moment.

When it happens the '*time-count*' - as set by God', will be initiated, giving our planet and us seven years to the end, as revealed in the Jewish Bible in the Book of Daniel 9:27.

In the Book of Revelation 11:2 and 1:5, the last three and a half years or forty-two months of the seven years is mentioned, as well.

God's '*revelations*' that HE would punish and eradicate mankind, because of our sinful living are close to beginning to be fulfilled - as HE foretold over and over.

His prophecies were warnings to mankind. But, Satan, our Nemesis, very skilfully got in the way preventing us from understanding them.

We have unfortunately been too busy to take time to listen to God.

One of the main purposes of this book - as indicated - is to provide awareness and consciousness of the need of mankind to change its by God unacceptable (wicked) ways.

Who am I to tell anybody what to do? My altruism is what drives me, my concern for the well-being of my same of kin. It's my hope that some of you will take action and turn to God asking for guidance, before it's too late!

## 8.4 THE IRREVERSIBLE DEVASTATING MAN-MADE GLOBAL WARMING

As we know, the man-made Poisonous Warming of the Atmosphere was initiated by the Industrialization in the mid 18-hundreds, when factories - as we can see in the Photograph – were set up and began to spew out rapidly increasing harmful emissions. And, it became worse and worse – with no reduction in sight - as the World became more and more industrialized; that accelerated enormously as the result of all the weapons that were manufactured during especially WWII.

Nobody had the slightest idea of what that black smoke was doing to the Atmosphere and to our planet, until very recently.

From: https://www.pinterest.com/sdace13/industrialization/

The photo gives an idea of what it looked like in many cities for many years emitting the greenhouse gases that unknown to all would change and warm up the Atmosphere.

It was the beginning, and being that nobody understood what was going on, we went on causing increasing damage to our previously clean Atmosphere.

Greed, avarice, materialism – the driving factors; nobody had the slightest idea of what we were causing - not just to the Atmosphere - but to our planet and to ourselves.

On top of it nobody realized – until recently - that the Atmosphere had been warming the Oceans, slowly, very slowly, invisible to our eyes, changing them irreversibly, forever!

Unfortunately, the new knowledge of the damaging '*inter-play*' that has been taking place between the Atmosphere and the Oceans is of no value - because the damage inflicted to the Oceans, warming them, has affected them '*beyond repair*'!

As I mentioned, '*the Industrialization*' is '*the most lethal weapon of mass destruction ever* created by man'. Its effects that have become known as the Global Warming or Climate Change is going to end up being far more devastating for our Planet, than if hundreds of A-Bombs were made to explode all at once.

It's a paradox that the same '*medium*' – *the Industrialization* - that made it possible to create so much well-being for mankind, is going to end up being the cause of its devastation.

In the Qur'an 102:1 God said,
**"O mankind, you have been distracted by the rivalry against each other of piling up worldly possessions."**

**Be sure that Satan thanks everybody for helping him.**

## 8.5 THE EFFECTS OF THE GLOBAL WARMING AFFECT PLANET EARTH

When I read 'scientific reports' that fill the Internet - relative to the Global Warming or Climate Change – the first impression they give – as I see it - is that Scientists present Planet Earth as it were a non-dynamic body, unaffected by variables.

But as I know now, our planet is a dynamic body, with the oceans that are very different in size and depth, forming - 'One Contiguous Body of Water' – that covers over two thirds of the planet's surface. It seems to me that this fact makes the planet prone to change its dynamics as the oceans change, pushed as they are by the constant increasing melt-waters that are distributed across the oceans, with the potential to reach different levels.

But, the most significant factor influencing the dynamics of our planet is the rotation around its 'imaginary axis.' The rotation creates the gravitation that produces a powerful pull of Gravitation and other factors.

The Article (By Harvard's Professor Jerry Mitrovica) titled, "The U.S. has caused more global warming than any other country. Here's how the Earth will get its revenge" (on the Internet 01/22/15) associated with the Link that follows, explains this matter in great detail.

http://www.washingtonpost.com/news/energy-environment/wp/2015/01/22/the-u-s-has-contributed-more-to-global-warming-than-any-other-country-heres-how-the-earth-will-get-its-revenge/

The vast melting Ice shelves in Antarctica and Greenland - as has been reported for many years - are releasing huge amounts of water that's distributed throughout the Oceans. What that does is to substantially add to their volume and weight – much more in some locations than in other – resulting principally from the pull of gravitation.

While this is happening - and as the gigantic Ice-structures are melting away - the weight over the bottom at the places where the ice melted away - are in an incessant decrease.

As the overlaying weight of the ice that pushed them down disappears, it turns out that the effect of it is that the ocean bottoms - are 'popping up' - making the surrounding waters less deep.

The important ensuing effect is that much more water becomes displaced, as reported – than just the melted waters - away to the oceans, speeding up the imbalance of our planet.

The Link provides insight on how it's happening in Iceland.

http://qz.com/336517/iceland-is-melting-so-fast-its-literally-popping-off-the-planet/

It's important to understand that *the problem* we're facing is the imbalance of the planet that's growing and is doing it with increasing speed, as I'm showing in the curve in sub-chapter1 8.11. It will continue to happen, as long as the ice-sheets and glaciers continue to melt and water is unevenly displaced around the planet.

It's curious that nothing is said by the Scientific Community about the damage that has been caused to the oceans. Instead, they uselessly continue concentrating on the need to reduce the emissions to the atmosphere.

Such a thing - the reduction of the emissions – will never happen anyhow because no country is doing anything of substance. But, even if all countries agreed to go ahead and do something, nothing can change the damage already in place – that's increasing incessantly.

Recent reports tell us that ocean beds are being pushed down by the rising waters. What this causes, is an added increase in the imbalance of the planet, and thereby in the wobble and instability of the rotation axis.

The planet's growing imbalance in turn, is causing the rotation axis to be pushed away, in search for a stable balanced rotation location. Which is what is in the process of causing extreme changes to the dynamics of our Planet, as we shall learn.

## 8.6 MEGA TSUNAMIS CAUSE DEVASTATION BEYOND IMAGINATION

Major underwater earthquakes are prone to cause Tsunamis, one of the most devastating of all Natural Phenomena. They occur when two tectonic plates, which are grinding against each other, suddenly come apart (rupture, as it has been called).

The most powerful earthquakes, those capable of triggering a Tsunami, occur at what are known as '*subduction zones*' where a plate is underneath the edge of an adjoining plate. Since there exist numerous subduction zones around the world, it's essential that we know the causes.

Links that describe what happened when the Sumatra Tsunami struck on December 26, 2004, just off the coast of the Indian Ocean – killing so many people around it.

http://www.tectonics.caltech.edu/outreach/highlights/sumatra/what.html

http://www.thehindu.com/sci-tech/what-caused-the-massive-2004-indian-ocean-tsunami/article6723085.ece

I provide them, so you can learn how our planet is behaving. Going out from Ancient Prophecies and the newer ones as well. In reality you don't need these Links, just type in 'Sumatra Tsunamis' and they come up.

There isn't the shade of a doubt that the triggering of much more devastating Tsunamis is at hand.

I want to return to Cayce's mention about the destruction of California and other places around the Planet. Those of you who check out the internet, I'm sure you have seen and read Articles that have appeared numerous times related to 'The Big One' in California, as it's called.

There exist three known large Faults along the West Coast, and the Links provide reports about each fault. What is it that makes the underwater Earthquakes to happen? There are different reasons, but one of them is for sure the added pressure that's applied to the Tectonic Plates from the rising water levels and thereby the weight of the same.

At some moment the added weight of the water atop will push a plate downwards, which will cause a Mega-Earthquake and the ensuing Tsunami. The greater the movement, the greater the Tsunami.

http://www.latimes.com/local/lanow/la-me-ln-san-andreas-fault-earthquake-20160504-story.html

https://en.wikipedia.org/wiki/San_Jacinto_Fault_Zone

http://news.yahoo.com/continental-collision-could-trigger-california-tsunami-140856981.html

It has been suggested that the San Andreas and San Jacinto faults could act together and cause a big devastation.

Then there's the 'Cascadian Subduction Zone' north thereof, very little known, but by far the worst threat of all, which as it seems, is overdue for a major earthquake. All of these are capable of causing the much mentioned 'Big One', especially if they become affected to hit all at once as has been suggested. It's a setup, to set off a disaster of cataclysmic proportion, such as mentioned by Cayce.

http://sf.curbed.com/archives/2015/07/13/omg_you_guys.php

Copied from the article in the Link that follows. [The Cascadian Subduction Zone is where an Earthquake will create 'Hell' – as the result of its ensuing Tsunami slamming into California]. In January in the Year 1700 a Tsunami, created Hell, in Japan, which was recorded. But it wasn't until very recently it has been found that the culprit was precisely the Cascadian Subduction zone, off the U.S. coast.

http://discovermagazine.com/2012/extreme-earth/01-big-one-earthquake-could-devastate-pacific-northwest

https://www.yahoo.com/news/pacific-northwest-may-most-risk-101002700.html

It's evident that the setting for the devastation that Cayce described for California has been set!

Given that the ice-melt is in an accelerating unstoppable process, the probability of it beginning to occur very soon, any day now, is very high.

When we take into account what Edgar Cayce said about the disappearance of New York City, a Tsunami is – as I see it – the most likely force that would make it happen. But wherefrom would it hit?

In the Spanish Canary Islands across the Atlantic Ocean, close to Africa, Cumbre Vieja is the largest volcano of several that poses a threat to the United States. Scientists fear that Cumbre Vieja, which erupted in 1949 and 1971, will erupt soon again.

Scientists warn there's a probability for a Tsunami to be caused by this Canary Island Volcano. This is because its upper half, it has been discovered (I've seen a documentary about it) is loose and can be made to fall into the Atlantic Ocean. An earthquake could cause it to collapse causing a Tsunami that would potentially wipe out the whole North American East Coast including New York City. Check out the two Links that follow.

http://www.independent.co.uk/travel/news-and-advice/canary-islands-volcano-eruption-tsunami-warning-cumbre-vieja-tenerife-a8018776.html

https://www.express.co.uk/news/science/866137/Canary-Islands-volcano-underwater-eruption-el-hierro-la-palma

Then there's the never mentioned Mid-Atlantic Ridge in the North Atlantic Ocean, about halfway between the US and Africa.

It's an underwater mountain chain that to date hasn't caused any problems, but going out from the mentioned prophecy of Cayce, is to be considered as a possible hazard for the causing of a potent Tsunami to impact the North American East Coast.

To all of this, I want to bring up what the Hopi have said – as mentioned in Sub-chapter 5.2 - about the matter of Tsunamis, when at the end *the oceans will join hands with the sky*!

## 8.7 "THE SUN WILL NO LONGER SHINE"… SAID GOD

Before getting into this subject, which I mentioned several times, I want to underline that Scientists cannot provide precise information of what's happening to our Planet because they lack *'the evidence of previous similar occurrences'*, upon which to base their predictions.

Therefore, Scientific Predictions about what's going on with our planet are to be viewed as assumptions without a trustworthy base. The Prophecies, on the other hand, are precise. By compiling all Prophecies – as I've done – we get a reasonably good idea about the time to the end.

Most important of all to have in mind, is what God has made clear, which is that as the result of His *'Furious Anger'* against mankind, HE will exterminate us.

Independently of what anybody wants to believe, it's 'a fact' that what God said – in His Prophecies or Revelations – was about for mankind fatal occurrences. Without the least doubt – they were – all of them - ominous (ill-omened) revelations (warnings) of God; that HE repeated many times in the Jewish Bible (Isaiah 13:10, 24:23 and 34:4 and later on through Joel 2:10, 2:31 and 3:14. They were again repeated in the Book of Revelation 6:12-14 and 16:20 that are the most severe of all His Prophecies.

HE repeated it in the Qur'an 81:1, wherein HE said, "*When the sun will no longer shine…*" How could it be that the powerful sun will cease to shine? The only explanation for such phenomena – as mentioned - is an extraordinary volcanic activity taking place all over our planet.

During the last years, there have been countless articles on the internet about more and more volcanoes that have become active and are erupting all around the planet.

In the following, a few Links and comments.

https://www.yahoo.com/news/experts-discuss-warning-signs-eruption-173941410.html

Experts Discuss Warning Signs of Eruption of Super Volcano at Yellowstone National Park.

The super-volcano in Yellowstone National Park may erupt sooner than previously expected, Scientists say. Experts believe the eruption would blanket most of the U.S. in ash, and send the earth into a volcanic ice age.

Volcanoes recently discovered under the ice in Antarctica.

https://www.yahoo.com/news/scientists-discover-91-volcanoes-slumbering-172136571.html

91 previously unknown volcanoes have been discovered underneath the West Antarctic ice-sheet. If verified through other studies, the new results would bring the total number of volcanoes beneath the ice-sheets in this part of Antarctica to nearly 140. It raises the unsettling possibility that sub-glacial heat from these volcanoes could speed up the melting of the ice.

https://www.scientificamerican.com/article/a-huge-plume-of-magma-is-bulging-against-antarctica/

https://www.forbes.com/sites/trevornace/2017/11/08/massive-heat-source-was-just-discovered-under-antarctica-driving-melting-volcanism/#493f29c0346d

https://www.forbes.com/sites/trevornace/2017/11/01/experts-warn-icelands-biggest-volcano-is-ready-to-erupt/#7fe215aa1f0c

https://www.forbes.com/sites/trevornace/2017/11/01/experts-warn-icelands-biggest-volcano-is-ready-to-erupt/#7fe215aa1f0c

Geologists are closely monitoring Iceland's biggest volcano after a string of recent activity. The earthquake activity is often a telltale sign that the volcano is preparing to erupt once again.

The Bardarbunga volcano is 6,590 feet tall and lies hidden beneath the Vatnajökull glacier, making it difficult to monitor directly beyond a few acoustic measurements. A geophysicist studying the volcano and based out of the University of Iceland believes recent activity is the result of the volcano filling its magma chamber in preparation for an eruption.

Lava flowing out of the Bardarbunga volcano in southeast Iceland. (Credit: Bernard Meric/AFP/Getty Images)

The Sakurajima, one of several volcanoes in Japan erupts spectacularly, filling the skies with black ashes.

Volcano Bogoslof, one of many volcanoes in the Alaska Aleutian Islands erupts, sending heavy ashes 35,000 feet into the air.

This gives a pre-view Scenario of how our skies will look more and more in a near future, as was repeatedly foretold by God in the Jewish Bible. It's evident that Planet Earth is preparing itself for what God foretold about, so many times.

## Indonesia's Sinabung volcano erupts, unleashes towering ash column

http://www.foxnews.com/world/indonesias-sinabung-volcano-erupts-unleashes-towering-ash-Column.html?utm_source=feedburner&utm_medium=feed&utm_campaign=Feed%3A+foxnews%2Fworld+%28Internal+-+World+Latest+-+Text%29

JAKARTA, Indonesia – Mount Sinabung on the Indonesian island of Sumatra shot billowing columns of ash more than 16,400 feet into the atmosphere and hot clouds down its slopes.

The Pacific's "Ring of Fire" is a breeding ground for natural disasters. Here's a look at the most recent incidents.

There were no fatalities or injuries from the morning eruption, the National Disaster Mitigation Agency said.

The volcano, one of three currently erupting in Indonesia, was dormant for four centuries before exploding killing two people. Another eruption killed 16 people, while seven died in a third eruption.

Mount Sinabung spews volcanic ash as it erupts in Kutarakyat, North Sumatra, Indonesia, (AP Photo/Endro Rusharyanto)

I could add any quantity of photos and Links related to Volcanoes that are either erupting or getting ready to become active and spew out tons of ashes that will darken the skies, making the sun to cease to shine, as the End-of-Our-Time is closing in on us.

A Volcano that's emerging from the seafloor in the Caribbean is quite unique, given that there aren't any known volcanoes in that area.

**Unique Caribbean underwater volcano showing seismic activity**

https://www.upi.com/Caribbean-ships-warned-away-from-underwater-volcano/7841521050446/

Photo courtesy Trinidad and Tobago Weather Center

I view it as an additional indication of global volcano activity adding to the Prophecies telling us that '*the sun will no longer be seen*'.

## 8.8 THE ONGOING DESTABILIZATION OF PLANET EARTH

As we've been learning, our planet is experiencing great upheavals and transformations, resulting from the vast ice-sheets in mainly Antarctica and Greenland, which are melting at an ever-increasing speed. The colossal volumes and weight of the melted water masses are being re-distributed all over the oceans.

Because the water is unevenly distributed as the result of mainly the Gravitational forces, a continuously growing imbalance is being caused to the planet, affecting its dynamics and the rotation.

This, in turn, is forcefully pushing the Earth's Rotation Axis seeking to find a stable point of rotation. As the melt water volumes increase and spread out, there's no way of stopping the ongoing imbalance increase.

Recent major earthquakes in Sumatra, Chile, and Japan affected, even if very minimally, caused the location of the Earth's Rotation Axis to be shifted, as described in Reports related to those occurrences you can easily find on the Internet.

As was reported, the magnitude 9.0 earthquake that struck Japan in March 2011 was powerful enough to shorten the day by 1.8 microseconds and throw an extra 17 centimeters (6.7 inches) into the planet's wobble. This is in addition to the earlier added centimeters (inches) that resulted from the earthquakes in 2004 off Sumatra, which added 7 cm and in Chile in 2010 that shifted the Earth's axis about 8 cm. As can be observed, for the Japan earthquake, the change in Earth's wobble was more than twice as large as those calculated for the 2004 and 2010 quakes.

The result will be that every time new powerful earthquakes happen the axis will be shifted. Now, then imagine what will occur when earthquakes become more frequent and more powerful.

As it is, Planet Earth naturally wobbles slightly as it spins. This is the result of shifting surface mass such as the melting ice-sheets at the poles and a multitude of glaciers and of changing ocean currents, which are throwing Planet Earth off balance.

Researchers are intrigued by the changing earth's wobble. The explanation is, as I believe, it's happening as the result of the already existing imbalance of Planet Earth – that's increasing as the result of the continuously added water masses; the ones that as we've found, become unevenly distributed around our planet.

## 8.9 MAJOR DESASTERS DESTROY POWERLINES ACROSS THE USA AND ALL OVER THE WORLD.

Edgar Cayce said many things about major earthquakes to cause great destruction around our planet, and change the shape of the North American Continent. But nobody gave importance to what he said.

However, when we see what's happening to our planet, I suggest it's high time to take very seriously and re-visit what Cayce said.

When we go out from Cayce's map, we realize that there are going to be many enormously destructive Earthquakes that – it's obvious - will destroy power lines in addition to so much more.

It will leave densely populated areas without electricity. Those power lines will never be repaired because money will be scarcer as new disasters happen all around. Without power all services will die, creating countless catastrophic situations and chaos.

This is due to occur in our generation and not in a distant future. So, maybe the concept of electric cars isn't that good after all. The idea is great, but hardly in such a scenario.

Gasoline will be in short supply, but it's transportable. However, what will happen to the power lines will also affect refineries. Most of them are found on the coasts, where rising water levels sooner or later will make them inoperable. Gas pumps at Gas stations will not function because there's no electricity.

We can also figure out that gasoline and gas ducts, will be destroyed or not have anything to transport.

If you don't believe in this kind of scenarios that's Okay. But, unfortunately, with the effects of the Global Warming speeding up, as they are, it's a matter of time – and I say, very short time – before these scenarios become commonplace.

I must say I'm truly sorry I'm not an Orson Wells who imagined fantastic scenarios of the future. Many of his – what seemed to be unrealistic ideas - came to happen.

God's Prophecies, unfortunately, don't offer any future.

## 8.10 THE 'COLLAPSE' OF THE GPS SATELLITE SYSTEM

On top of the widespread destruction described, the GPS or 'Global Position Satellite' system, used in many important applications is due to become inoperable.

The Satellites are 'stationary', meaning that they are in 'fixed' locations in space relative to the Earth. But, if the planet's current rotation pattern changes - as it is in the process of doing – the locations of the Satellites as viewed from earth will seem to move and lose their inter-related synchronization. This will make the GPS system to collapse, making it unusable.

We can understand how exact the System Requirement is when we learn that the GPS System uses Atomic Clocks. All of that will result useless when the Satellites, as indicated, go out of Synch with the planet.

To determine the exact location of anything on the ground, it's necessary to have four GPS Satellites 'in sight' synchronized with each other. It's therefore easy to understand that when the planet becomes forced to move out of position - as described - the exactness of the GPS Global System becomes lost.

Nobody will want to accept that such a scenario is possible, but the reality is that this is what will soon happen, unless the accelerating ice-melt becomes stopped, which it can't. As a result, a host of Systems using GPS will get *out-of-sync* which will cause havoc. But those who take precautionary measures may be able to avoid some of the unfolding chaos.

To give an idea of what I know about Radio, I graduated as a Radio Engineer, and worked among others, with the service, maintenance, testing and retrofitting of Radio, Sonar and Radar systems in the Swedish Royal Navy, and at Philips with TV. As mentioned in my introduction, I became an expert on the Cellular Radio-Telephone Systems as well.

With the GPS out of Synch, Cellular Systems that use GPS in the Hand-off or Hand-over of conversations between the Cells – for people moving around in vehicles – and in micro-cell systems – there will be trouble.

The question is if airplanes and ships will be able to navigate without the GPS?

## 8.11 EXPONENTIALLY RISING CURVE SHOWS THE TIME LEFT

What does the Curve show? The Curve depicts the Likely Approximate Exponential *'Ice-melt-rate-increase'* of the Vast Ice-Sheets in mainly Antarctica and Greenland over the next few years, as has been reported on the Internet. It is an irreversible accelerating process that is de-stabilizing the Balance and the Gravity of Planet Earth!

How is it possible to define the exact time for the End from this Moment? There's one Prophecy in the Book of Daniel in the Jewish Bible that describes a unique occurrence that is to take place in the Middle East at any moment.

When it happens, *'the time-clock for our last seven years – a time that has been set by God, as revealed - begins to tick'*.

Everything that's happening to our planet and to mankind is intimately interrelated and can't be changed.

The scenario for what's on course to happen is reaching completion. There's the unique occurrence that provides the starting point, pending to take place at any moment; there are the seven last years, to reach the end; and there are the effects of the Global Warming accelerating ahead with relentlessly increasing speed – until reaching the end - our unfortunate destiny.

Please note that I created the curve to get an idea of the increasing amount of ice – *in Billions of Metric Tons per year* - that's melting. I merely took the curve with our current date and added the seven years, the beginning of which is pending – that will provide the end date.

As we've learned, what's taking place with our planet was foretold by God in the Jewish Bible and again in the Book of Revelation, and HE confirms it again in the Qur'an.

The Seven (3½ + 3½) last years are mentioned in one more Prophecy in the Book of Revelation without giving a time-frame.

Please note that there does not exist a nexus or 'connection' per se between the melt-waters and the Prophecies. I took the information contained in the Prophecies and made the necessary 'connection'.

It's not a matter of magic, but of my using the scientific knowledge I've acquired tying it into the Prophecies, and applied 'Common Sense'.

## 8.12 MOUNTAINS AND ISLANDS SUDDENLY DISAPPEAR

What's said in this heading is a revelation that tells exactly how the end will take place.

As we learned from Harvard Scientist Noemi Oreskes in the Article mentioned before, Earth Scientists have taken 'distance' to religion. Since the Prophecies are part of a religion, Scientists missed out on the teachings found in the Jewish Bible, wherein God revealed what would happen to our planet.

Learning about the Prophecies wouldn't have changed anything, but maybe, just maybe, the Scientists could have had a different understanding of what's going on. As mentioned before, I believe that the rejection on part of the Earth Scientific Community to have anything to do with His many End-of-Time prophecies in the Jewish Bible must have been an offence to God, who, as I see it, put in a great effort to provide the mass of information they contain, as I'm describing it in this Book.

Before continuing, a few words about our planet. The equatorial circumference is about 40,000 Kilometers or 24,900 Miles. This means that the speed with which it rotates – to make one turn around itself in 24 hours - is about 1,670 Kilometers or 1000 Miles per hour. Very fast, in other words.

The reason to bring in these data is to enable us to get an understanding of the havoc that will take place when the planet suddenly falls (tilts) over, changing the direction of its rotation.

All of the sudden colossal forces will begin to re-landscape our planet's surface. This will be the moment when the mountains and islands suddenly disappear. It was at the previous tilting that all the existing Mountain Ranges came into being.

It will be when what's revealed through John from Patmos in the Book of Revelation in revelations 6 and 16, takes place when *every mountain and island become removed from its place.*

This is what will occur at the tilting when the Tectonic Plates/ Continents are forced to move apart, or collide against each other with colossal force as will occur when the Planet suddenly falls away from its current rotation direction.

That's the moment when all mountain ranges, such as the Himalayans in Asia, the Rocky Mountains in the U.S.A., the Andes in Latin America and all other will disappear, as God foretold long time ago would happen.

The tilting will cause cataclysmic disasters, as none before, such as Cayce said would occur in our time when he said that the planet was going to tilt over.

At the coming tilting - foretold many times - all Mountains will fall back into the seas, and new ones will come into being.

This is to give an idea of what it is that will happen. When, the '*the heavens receded*,' it is that the skies will look that way, when the planet falls over itself.

In the Book of Revelation 6:12-14 it's said that there *will be a great earthquake. The stars* (will look as if they) were *falling to earth, as ripe figs drop from a fig tree in a strong storm.*' When this happens, *the heavens will* (seem to) *recede like a scroll being rolled up.*

This and what's written below, are clear-cut descriptions of what will happen when the Rotation Axis, seeking its new balanced equilibrium – causes the overturn of Planet Earth.

The overturning (tipping over or collapse) of our planet – '*The Final Effect of devastation*' caused by the Global Warming – was foretold by God in a multitude of Revelations in the Jewish Bible before the revelations that were given to John.

In the Qur'an, God brought up this subject that sounds familiar when compared to the ones from the Bible.

In Qur'an 77:7-10 it's said that *the mountains will be blown away.* In Qur'an 78:19-20 it's said that *the disappearing mountains will make it seem as they had been an illusion.*

As we've learned, the Global Warming of the Atmosphere has warmed and changed the Oceans. The warmed Oceans, in turn, are in the process of melting the vast ice-sheets at the Poles, and a multitude of glaciers. While the weight at the '*Melt–locations*' are reducing their weight, the '*Melt-waters*' being dispersed are increasing the weight of the Oceans unevenly.

All of this - as mentioned – which is of fundamental importance to understand - is in the process of creating '*a rapidly growing imbalance to our planet*' – that directly affects the point of equilibrium of the Rotation Axis.

We've learned that every time there was a major Earthquake, like the ones in Japan, in Sumatra and Chile, the Rotation Axis became displaced, minimally yes, but it happened.

Reports related to the Global Warming affecting the Oceans swarm the Internet. They provide clear-cut evidence that our planet is in dear trouble; because - there's nothing that can be done to reverse the harm that mankind has caused to the warmed-up oceans. That, in turn has caused the melting of the vast Ice-sheets in Antarctica and in Greenland that's in advanced process of bringing catastrophe to our planet.

As we know – no secret - the emitted man-made pollutants have continually been increasing at an ever more accelerated rate. The '*Cause & Effect*' products of the contamination of the Atmosphere and the resulting warming are equally in the process of an exponentially increasing acceleration, producing additional harmful effects – that are affecting the oceans.

In addition to this, there are the Millions of tons of poisonous Methane gases being released and added to the Atmosphere, as deep-frozen permafrost lands and ocean-bottoms are increasingly de-frosting at countless locations, as reported on the Internet.

This, in turn, is warming up the Atmosphere even more, accelerating the melting of the vast ice-sheets in mainly Antarctica and Greenland, and consequently the rise of the levels of the Oceans.

But, the most pressing matter, as mentioned so many times, and must be mentioned again, is how this is affecting the uneven increase in volume and weight of the Oceans; '*that's causing an irreversible growing imbalance to our planet*', which in turn is affecting the equilibrium of the Rotation Axis.

When, many years ago, I read the above Prophecies and also what Edgar Cayce had said that the planet would overturn, I began to pay attention to how mountains were formed. I have driven to many distant locations and found, as I drove through many roads cut out through mountains – they all show ascending inclinations along their sides - providing evidence that they must have been pushed upwards. On the Island of Curaçao just off the coast of Venezuela, I observed that the formation of its small mountains provides the best evidence of a sudden violent push upwards than anywhere I had ever seen before.

Something that called my attention early on was the many findings of marine fossils found on top of the highest mountains, such as on Mount Everest. This provides irrefutable evidence that today's Mountain Ranges (the ones that God prophesized will disappear) once were down at the Sea level. The Tectonic Plates were pushed up with colossal force at the previous tilting, thus forming the current Mountain ranges.

Only the tilting of Planet Earth could have caused such a cataclysmic change to take place, and there isn't any doubt that it happened several times in the past, for whatever reasons.

Independently of what caused the former tilting, it's obvious that the reason why it happened must have been an imbalance of our planet that grew until it caused the Rotation Axis to seek a new stable equilibrium. And, that's precisely what's on course to happen now.

I find it astonishing that Scientists have their discussions about the rising seas, but not once – as far as I'm aware - has anybody issued a warning about the increasing imbalance of the planet and that it will cause it to collapse. The question to be made is when will it happen?

The approximate time - it is on course to happen very soon – in our generation!

## 8.13 THE PROPHESIED FALLING STARS - AN OPTICAL ILLUSION

In Isaiah 34:4 and in Revelation 6:13, is written – a repeat, '*The stars fell down to the earth...*'

What does this mean? Is it really possible for stars – gigantic suns - which are light years of distance away and light years away from each other - to fall down on our planet and, at the same time? It would take light-years for them to reach our planet.

At issue is if anybody is going to be alive looking at the impenetrably dark skies and be able to see what happens.

The Prophecy in Isaiah 34:4 continues '*and the sky disappeared like a scroll being rolled up*'.

This tells us that something is happening to our planet. It will depend on how we stand in regards to how we see what will be taking place; and as I see it there'll be two different scenarios.

If I stand such that the planet is flipping backwards behind me, the optical illusion I'll get is as if '*the stars are falling*' on the earth (our planet), as Isaiah wrote.

But if I turn around and look the other way, the optical illusion of the sky will be that of '*shooting stars*' rushing away when the planet flips forward.

The distant stars will continue being light years away. None of them will have moved. Our planet however, will have changed in many ways. The most important is that God will make human and animal life to disappear forever, as HE foretold very clearly through His Prophet Zephaniah.

# 8.14 HE (GOD) IS THE LORD OF THE TWO EASTS AND THE TWO WESTS

In Qur'an 55:17 it's written, 'HE (God) is the LORD (the Owner) of the two easts and the LORD of the two wests.'

Up to this point, nobody has been able to understand what's meant by this odd mention.

But, what's said, ties perfectly well in with what will occur after the tipping over of the planet.

*Because after it's all over*, Planet Earth will be rotating in a different orientation.

Sunrise will therefore occur in what will be '*a new East* ' and Sunset will take place in '*a new West*', confirming that HE is the LORD of the two Easts (the current one and a new) and the LORD of two Wests (the current one and a new).

# FINAL WORDS

The End is Looming — Judgment Day, the Day of Regret
for many or most human beings is nearing, as foretold by Almighty God.
Can anything be made to prevent the foretold devastation of our planet?
The answer is. Nothing can be done to change what God Prophesied.
But, there's One thing that can be changed,
which is the behaviour and actions of each one of us.
Working to Save my Soul is the #1 Task.
This Book provides guidance
to learn what we need to do and change
in order to be able to find and please God!
Believe in the only Living God and have faith in Him.
Strictly Obey His Commandments!
Turn to Him in prayer and ask for forgiveness for your sins.
If you do it in your Heart, HE will know!
It is the First Step towards trying to secure for yourself
a place in the Kingdom of the only Living God!
He is the All-seeing, All-knowing, All-wise, All-aware,
the Compassionate, the Merciful, the Forgiving!
It is HE Who is, Who was, Who will continue to live forever!
I hope that learning from this Book will be of help to you
to make the necessary changes,
to be accepted into the Kingdom of God.

**— THE END —**

# INDEX

## CHAPTER 7

## CHAPTER 8

## FINAL WORDS [163]

www.ingramcontent.com/pod-product-compliance
Lightning Source LLC
Chambersburg PA
CBHW052112030426
42335CB00025B/2954